asian
twist

A CONTEMPORARY TASTE OF EAST MEETS WEST

asian
twist

A CONTEMPORARY TASTE OF EAST MEETS WEST

KEVIN LIM

Marshall Cavendish
Cuisine

The Publisher wishes to thank **Parkson Grand, KLCC,** Malaysia and **Living Quarters Sdn Bhd,** Malaysia for the loan of their crockery and utensils.

Editor : Yeo Puay Khoon
Art Direction/Designer : Christopher Wong
Photographer : Edmond Ho
Prop Stylists : Christopher Wong, Christine Chong and
Joycelyn George

Published by Marshall Cavendish Cuisine
An imprint of Marshall Cavendish International (Asia) Private Limited
A member of the Times Publishing Limited
Times Centre, 1 New Industrial Road, Singapore 536196
Tel: (65) 6213 9288   Fax: (65) 6285 4871
E-mail: te@sg.marshallcavendish.com
Online Bookstore: http://www.marshallcavendish.com/genref

Malaysian Office:
Federal Publications Sdn Berhad (General & Reference Publishing)
(3024-D)
Times Subang, Lot 46, Persiaran Teknologi Subang
Subang Hi-Tech Industrial Park, Batu Tiga, 40000 Shah Alam
Selangor Darul Ehsan, Malaysia
Tel: (603) 5635 2191   Fax: (603) 5635 2706
E-mail: cchong@tpg.com.my

National Library Board (Singapore) Cataloguing in Publication Data

Lim, Kevin, 1971-
Asian twist :a contemporary taste of East meets West / [chef, Kevin Lim]. – Singapore :Marshall Cavendish Cuisine, c2004.
p. cm.

ISBN : 981-232-695-2

1.   Cookery, Asian. I. Title.

TX724.5.A1
641.595 — dc21   SLS2004085317

Printed in Singapore by Fabulous Printers Pte Ltd

This book is dedicated, in loving memory, to my mother, Madam See Kean Sim, for her guidance, inspiration and devotion and for helping me to achieve my dreams.

1. Mr Patrick Ng, Managing Director of Potterhaus Singapore, for his creative handmade glassware.

... my lovely family for their support ... encouragement.

CONTENTS

Preface • 20
Glossary • 188
Weights & Measures • 192

CONTENTS

CONTENTS

CONTENTS

CONTENTS

CONTENTS

CONTENTS

CONTENTS

Someone once asked me the definition of food. Without hesitation, my answer was "Food is like fashion, it's a trend".

In other words, it is flexible and innovative, and it is an adventure. To experience food, one has to be open and test the limits but fundamentally, I believe one has to understand of the strengths and weaknesses of one's ingredients.

My love for food started at an early age. At home with my mother, the food was never extravagant, but it always tasted good. I may not have realised it then, but I know now that I appreciate good food and flavours because of these early experiences.

Furthermore, being a Malaysian who has been exposed to the choice of food available in our multi-racial society as well as having undergone years of culinary training in various five-star hotels, cooking competitions and trips overseas, I have been inspired to explore and experiment passionately to create contemporary cuisine.

With this book, I would like to share with you the wonders of a uniquely prepared cuisine that represents a glorious and delicious mixture of many cultures.

Chef Kevin Lim

APPETIZER

asian
twist

TROUT TARTARE

SERVED WITH HONEY-HORSERADISH SAUCE

INGREDIENTS

Salmon trout fillets
240 g, finely chopped

Coriander (cilantro)
15 g, finely sliced

Freshly crushed black peppercorns
2 pinches

Salt
a pinch

Lemon juice
2 Tbsp

Sesame lavosh, prepared
4 portions

Hard-boiled eggs, whites
3, finely chopped

Honeydew melon
200 g, cut into small cubes

Honey-Horseradish Sauce
Horseradish
15 g

Honey
15 g

Mayonnaise
100 g

Cream
1 Tbsp

Salt
to taste

Pepper
to taste

Sugar
to taste

Garnish
Salmon roe
40 g

METHOD

- Combine ready chopped salmon trout, Chinese parsley, black peppercorns, salt and lemon juice in a bowl. Toss well and keep chilled to marinate for 20 minutes.

- To prepare Honey-Horseradish Sauce, combine horseradish, honey, mayonnaise and cream in a salad bowl. Stir well with a whisk, add salt, pepper and sugar to taste. Keep chilled for use later.

- Place a piece of sesame lavosh and put a spoonful of chopped egg white onto it and spread evenly. Place the second piece of sesame lavosh then spread marinated salmon trout onto it. Place the third piece of sesame lavosh and top with honeydew melon cubes.

- Drizzle on Honey-Horseradish Sauce and garnish with salmon roe.

Chicken

FLOSS CAESAR SALAD

INGREDIENTS

Romaine (cos) lettuce
320 g

Extra Virgin olive oil
80 ml

Salt
to taste

Lemon juice
to taste

Garlic
30 g, peeled and crushed

Anchovy fillets
20 g

Worcestershire sauce
1 tsp

Dijon mustard
20 g

Tabasco sauce
2 drops

Chopped parsley
1 tsp

Freshly crushed black peppercorns
a pinch

Sun-dried tomatoes
60 g

Hard-boiled eggs, yolks
4

Garnish
Grated Parmesan cheese
2 Tbsp

Pesto croutons
20 g

Chicken floss
60 g

METHOD

- Place Romaine lettuce in a bowl and cut with knife and fork. Keep on the side.

- In a large wooden bowl, sprinkle a little salt. Add lemon juice to dissolve salt.

- Crush cloves of garlic and anchovy fillets finely with a fork.

- Add Worcestershire sauce, Dijon mustard, Tabasco sauce, chopped parsley and crushed black peppercorns.

- Toss the dressing with Romaine lettuce, sun-dried tomatoes and egg yolks.

- Garnish with grated Parmesan cheese, pesto croutons and chicken floss.

INGREDIENTS

Shallots
30 g, peeled and finely sliced

Torch ginger bud (*Bunga kantan*)
1/2, finely chopped

Lemon grass
15 g, finely chopped

Coriander (cilantro)
8 g, finely sliced

Polygonum (*laksa*) leaves
2 stalks, finely sliced

Lemon juice
2 Tbsp

Fish sauce
to taste

Sugar
to taste

Sesame oil
1/2 tsp

Scallops
160 g

Mango, unripe
1/2, julienned

Japanese cucumber, sliced
40 g

Horseradish Potato
Russet potatoes
150 g, boiled and cut into small cubes

Mayonnaise
50 g

Horseradish
15 g

Salt
to taste

Freshly crushed black peppercorns
a pinch

Mint and Chilli Vinaigrette
Olive oil
80 ml

Mint leaves
10 g, finely sliced

Red chillies
15 g, finely chopped

Champagne vinegar
1 Tbsp

Sugar
to taste

Garnish
Edible flowers

METHOD

- Combine shallots, torch ginger bud, lemon grass, coriander, polygonum leaves, lemon juice, fish sauce, sugar and sesame oil in a bowl. Toss well.

- Add scallops and julienned mango, toss again and marinate overnight in the refrigerator.

- To prepare Horseradish Potato, mix well boiled potato, mayonnaise and horseradish in a salad bowl. Adjust with salt and pepper then keep chilled.

- To prepare Mint and Chilli Vinaigrette, combine olive oil, mint leaves, chillies and champagne vinegar. Add seasoning to taste.

- To serve, place the marinated scallop onto a plate and top with Horseradish Potato. Wrap sliced cucumber around the potato. Drizzle with Mint and Chilli Vinaigrette.

- Garnish with edible flowers.

Ceviche

SCALLOPS "KERABU STYLE"

FRESH SCALLOP, MARINATED WITH LEMON JUICE, CORIANDER AND SESAME OIL

Asian CAPRESE
THIN SLICES OF ROMA TOMATOES, BEAN CURD AND FRESH MINT WITH BALSAMIC-SHOYU VINAIGRETTE

INGREDIENTS

Roma tomatoes
2, sliced

Japanese bean curd, white
1 tube, sliced

Fresh mint leaves
10 g

Freshly crushed black peppercorns
4 pinches

Balsamic-Shoyu Vinaigrette
Olive oil
40 ml

Balsamic vinegar
60 ml

Light soy sauce
20 ml

Salt
a pinch

Freshly crushed black peppercorns
a pinch

Grated white radish
1/2 Tbsp

Ginger juice
1/2 tsp

Garnish
Finely sliced spring onions

METHOD

- To make Balsamic-Shoyu Vinaigrette, mix well all the ingredients and keep chilled for 1 hour. Strain.
- Arrange sliced tomatoes, bean curd and fresh mint leaves on a plate.
- Sprinkle with freshly crushed black peppercorns.
- Drizzle with Balsamic-Shoyu Vinaigrette before serving.
- Garnish with spring onions.

31

INGREDIENTS

Raisins
30 g, soaked in orange juice

Orange juice
100 ml

Romaine lettuce
200 g, sliced into 2.5-cm lengthways

Sunflower seeds
20 g, roasted

Cherry tomatoes
80 g, halved

Unripe mango
80 g, julienned

Mayonnaise
100 g

Plain yoghurt
100 g

Orange juice
40 ml

Lemon juice
2 Tbsp

Sugar
2 tsp

Eel (*Unagi*)
200 g, cut into 1.5 x 9-cm sticks

***Tempura* batter**
300 g

Cooking oil
1 litre, for deep-frying

Romaine

RAISIN, SUNFLOWER SEED AND UNAGI SALAD

SERVED WITH FRUIT DRESSING

METHOD

- Soak raisins in 100 ml orange juice for ¹/₂ hour then set aside.

- Combine Romaine lettuce, sunflower seeds, cherry tomatoes, raisins and julienned mango.

- Stir-well mayonnaise with yoghurt, orange juice, lemon juice and sugar to taste. Keep chilled.

- Dip unagi into the *tempura* batter and deep-fry until golden brown.

- Serve with tossed salad and drizzle with fruit dressing.

INGREDIENTS

Salmon fillet
240 g, cut into 20 g slices

Malay Ulam Salad
Ulam raja
20 g

Pucuk paku
20 g

Daun selom
20 g

Coriander (cilantro)
10 g

Mint leaf
10 g

Cucumber
50 g, julienned

Spicy Sour Plum Dressing
Sour plum sauce
100 g

Sour plum
50 g

Kalamansi juice
15 ml

Torch ginger bud (*Bunga kantan*)
10 g, finely chopped

Coriander (cilantro)
5 g, finely chopped

Garlic
12 g, peeled and finely chopped

Bird's eye chillies
5 g, finely chopped

***Tom Yam* paste**
10 g

Sugar
to taste

Garnish
Deep-fried bee hoon
4 portions

Salmon

CARPACCIO
FRESHLY SLICED SALMON FILLET SERVED WITH TRADITIONAL MALAY ULAM AND SPICY SOUR PLUM DRESSING

METHOD

- To prepare Malay Ulam Salad, toss all the salad ingredients together well then keep chilled.
- To make Spicy Sour Plum Dressing, combine all the dressing ingredients and mix well.
- Place sliced salmon on a plate then top with a mixture of Malay Ulam Salad.
- Drizzle the dressing over the salmon sashimi and garnish with deep-fried bee hoon.

Fresh

MUSHROOM AND EDAMAME BRUSCHETTA

TOASTED BREAD TOPPED WITH
SAUTEED MUSHROOMS AND EDAMAME

INGREDIENTS

Herb Oil*
20 g

French loaf or Ciabatta
4 portions, cut in 1-cm thick slices

Garlic
30 g, peeled and chopped

Onions
20 g, peeled and chopped

Freshly crushed black peppercorn
2 pinches

Shiitake mushrooms
100 g, cubed

Fresh button mushrooms
60 g, peeled and sliced

**Green vegetable soy beans
(Edamame)**
100 g

Roma tomatoes
100 g, cubed

White wine (optional)
1 Tbsp

Salt
to taste

***Herb Oil**

Fresh parsley
10 g

Fresh watercress leaves
10 g

Fresh basil
6 leaves

Fresh rosemary
1 g

Fresh thyme
1 g

Dried oregano flakes
a pinch

Dried tarragon flakes
a pinch

Dried marjoram flakes
a pinch

Olive oil
60 ml

METHOD

- To make Herb Oil, wash the parsley and watercress then drain.

- Place basil, rosemary, thyme, parsley, watercress, oregano, tarragon and marjoram flakes into a food processor.

- Blend the mixed herbs and pour in the olive oil slowly into the food processor. Blend until fine. Remove and keep chilled.

- Dip a pastry brush into the prepared Herb Oil and brush the surface of the sliced French loaf or Ciabatta. Place slices under a salamander or oven to toast.

- Heat oil in a non-stick pan, sauté chopped garlic, onion and freshly crushed black peppercorns until aromatic.

- Add in mushrooms and green vegetable soy beans to fry, followed by Roma tomatoes.

- Deglaze with white wine.

- Add salt to taste.

- Serve the mushroom mixture on the toasted bread.

INGREDIENTS

Mesclun mix salad
20 g

Sea bass
300 g, preferably use live sea bass

Laksa Marinade
Dried chilli
10 g

Lemon grass
2 stalks

Torch ginger bud (*Bunga kantan*)
$^1/_2$

Galangal
10 g, skinned

Fresh turmeric
10 g, skinned

Shallots
20 g, peeled

Black fermented prawn paste (*Rojak*) sauce
30 g

Tamarind juice
1 Tbsp

Polygonum (*laksa*) leaves
10 g

Sugar
2 Tbsp

Water
3 Tbsp

Salt
to taste

Avocado Salsa
Avocado
100 g, cut into small cubes

Roma tomatoes
60 g, cut into small cubes

Ripe mango
60 g, cut into small cubes

Water chestnut
40 g, cut into small cubes

Coriander (cilantro)
1 sprig, finely sliced

Lemon
$^1/_2$, juiced

Lemon-Herb Oil
Lemon juice
80 ml

Olive oil
40 ml

Mixed herbs
15 g

Salt
to taste

Freshly crushed black pepper
to taste

Ginger-Coconut Cream
Fresh coconut milk
70 ml

Mayonnaise
20 g

Grated ginger
10 g

Sugar
to taste

Garnish
Hanaho

METHOD

- Clean and fillet the sea bass then set aside.
- To make the Laksa Marinade, combine all marinade ingredients and put it into a food processor. Blend until fine.
- Place the sea bass fillets into a bowl. Pour the Laksa Marinade over, covering the fillets entirely.
- Keep in the chiller to marinate for 5 hours.
- To make Avocado Salsa, combine all salsa ingredients and stir well. Set aside for use later.
- For Lemon-Herb Oil, combine all lemon-herb oil ingredients and stir with a whisk until well mixed.
- For Ginger-Coconut Cream, combine all cream ingredients and stir with a whisk until well mixed. Keep chilled.
- To serve, thinly slice the marinated sea bass, place on a plate and garnish with Avocado Salsa and *hanaho*.
- Drizzle with Lemon-Herb Oil and Ginger-Coconut Cream before serving.

Gravlax

OF SEA BASS

LAKSA-MARINATED SEA BASS
FILLET SERVED WITH GINGER-
COCONUT CREAM,
AVOCADO SALSA AND
LEMON HERB OIL

INGREDIENTS

Soft shell crabs
4

Tempura **flour**
50 g

Tempura **batter**
400 g

Spicy Mango and Apple Salad
Unripe mango
80 g, peeled and cut into matchsticks

Green apple
80 g, peeled and cut into matchsticks

Thai chilli flakes
2 pinches

Lemon
$1/2$, juiced

Apple cider vinegar
$1/2$ Tbsp

Roasted cumin seeds
1 g

Sesame Dressing
Egg yolks
2

Soy bean oil
80 ml

Vinegar
20 ml

Shoyu
25 ml

Onion
20 g, peeled and grated

Garlic
10 g, peeled and grated

Japanese sesame oil
1 tsp

Roasted sesame seeds
35 g

Salt
a pinch

Sugar
$1/2$ tsp

Garnish
Japanese bamboo leaves
4

Frisee
4 portions

Sliced *hajikami*
1 tsp

METHOD

- To make Spicy Mango and Apple Salad, combine all salad ingredients. Toss well then set aside.

- Place egg yolks in a large salad bowl. Pour in soy bean oil and whisk with egg yolks to form an emulsion.

- Add in vinegar, *shoyu*, onion, garlic, sesame oil, sesame seeds, salt and sugar to taste. Set aside for use later.

- Heat oil in a large pot. Coat soft shell crabs with *tempura* flour, dash away the excess flour and dip into the *tempura* batter.

- Deep-fry the soft shell crabs until golden brown. Remove and drain away the oil.

- Serve the crispy soft shell crabs and Spicy Mango and Apple Salad with sesame dressing. Garnish with frisee and sliced *hajikami*.

Soft Shell

CRAB TEMPURA
SERVED WITH A SPICY SALAD OF
MANGO AND APPLE WITH A SESAME DRESSING

INGREDIENTS

Cream cheese
200 g, cubed

Japanese cucumber
30 g, thinly sliced

Miso Sauce
Preserved soy bean (*taucu*)
70 g, chopped

White *miso* paste
5 g

Pickled green chillies
70 g, chopped

Thai chilli flakes
2 pinches

Mirin
10 ml

Sugar
4 tsp

Garnish
Spring onions (scallions)
10 g, finely sliced

Cream
CHEESE WITH MISO

METHOD

- For *Miso* Sauce, mix all the sauce ingredients well and keep chilled.

- Place the cream cheese cubes on top of cucumber slices on a plate. Pour the *miso* sauce over and garnish with spring onions.

SASHIMI
WITH BRAISED
MUSHROOMS, GINGKO
NUTS AND CHESTNUTS

INGREDIENTS

US beef
250 g, thinly sliced

Butter
50 g

Garlic
8 g, peeled and chopped

Freshly crushed black peppercorn
2 pinches

Shiitake mushrooms
80 g

Shimeiji **mushrooms**
80 g

Enoki **mushrooms**
50 g

Chestnuts
30 g, boiled and diced

Grated ginger
1 tsp

Sake
1 Tbsp

Mirin
100 ml

Shoyu
to taste

Beef stock reduction
400 ml

Gingko nuts
30 g, boiled

Hondashi
to taste

Garnish
Fresh *Kaiware* (radish sprout)
4 portions

METHOD

- Place beef slices on a plate and keep chilled.

- Melt butter in pan, sauté garlic and crushed black peppercorn until fragrant then add in the mixture of mushrooms, chestnuts and grated ginger.

- Flambé with *sake* and *mirin*. Add in *shoyu* and beef stock reduction, stir well and simmer for 2–5 minutes.

- Add gingko nuts and season to taste with *hondashi*.

- To serve, place a piece of cling film onto a round mould. Layer with beef slices and fill with mixture of braised mushrooms. Press evenly and firmly.

- Turn over the mould onto a plate, remove the mould and cling film.

- Pour in the mushroom sauce before serving. Garnish with fresh *Kaiware*.

INGREDIENTS

Sushi Rice Vinegar
Short grain rice
350 g, cooked

Rice vinegar
100 ml

Mirin
35 ml

Salt
a pinch

Sugar
5 Tbsp

Pie Tee **Cup**
Wheat flour
100 g

Rice flour
100 g

Egg
200 g

Kapur (Sodium benzoic)
2 tsp

Water
300 ml

Toppings
Salmon
40 g, sliced

Tuna belly (*Toro*)
40 g, sliced

Salmon roe (*Ikura*)
4 tsp

Smoked eel (*Unagi*)
40 g, sliced

Chicken floss
20 g

Japanese bean curd
1

Octopus (*Tako*)
40 g, sliced

Caviar
10 g

Garnish
Black truffle
5 g

Chive
1 g

Wasabi tobiko
5 g

Cherry tomato
1

Miso **sauce**
2 tsp

METHOD

- To cook the rice, wash and rinse the rice in cold water. Repeat the process with changes of cold water until the water turns from cloudy to clear. Drain in a sieve. Then cook the rice in a rice cooker.

- Transfer the cooked rice into a wide shallow container. Mix the rice vinegar, *mirin*, salt and sugar together and pour the mixture into the rice quickly. Use a wooden spatula to toss the rice while it is still hot. Leave to cool. (Use 100 ml of rice vinegar for every 600 g of uncooked rice.)

- Stir all the *pie tee* cup ingredients together to form a batter and keep aside.

- Heat oil in wok and place the *pie tee* mould into the hot oil for 5 minutes.

- Remove from the hot oil and dip into the prepared *pie tee* batter. Take out and then place into the hot oil.

- Lightly shake the mould to loosen the crispy batter from the mould. Repeat the method until you have 16 *pie tee* cups. Place all the *pie tee* cups on absorbent paper.

- Fill the *pie tee* cups with Sushi rice and garnish with selection of toppings and garnishes.

Pie Tee

SUSHI

SUSHI RICE IN CRISPY GOLDEN
PIE TEE CUPS SERVED WITH A
VARIETY OF TOPPINGS

INGREDIENTS

Fresh beef liver
300 g, sliced

Sesame oil
3 tsp

Grated young ginger
1 tsp, skinned

Thai chilli flakes
3 pinches

Roasted sesame seeds
3 tsp

Spring onions (scallions)
30 g, finely sliced

Shoyu Dressing
Higashimaru Shoyu
25 ml

Mitsukan Suehiro Su (vinegar)
50 ml

Mirin
100 ml

***Bonito* flakes**
5 g

Fresh

BEEF LIVER SALAD

METHOD

- For *Shoyu* Dressing, mix all the dressing ingredients together then chill for 1 hour. Strain.

- Place the beef liver on a serving plate. Pour in the *Shoyu* Dressing, sesame oil and grated ginger.

- Sprinkle with Thai chilli flakes, roasted sesame seeds and spring onions.

SOUP

asian

twist

Mushroom

BISQUE
SERVED WITH CRISPY WANTON

INGREDIENTS

Butter
80 g

Onion
80 g, peeled and chopped

Garlic
30 g, peeled and chopped

Freshly crushed black peppercorns
$^1/_2$ tsp

Dried oregano
1 g

Fresh basil leaves
10 g

Dried marjoram
1 g

Fresh abalone mushrooms
300 g, sliced

Fresh Shiitake mushrooms
200 g, sliced

Fresh button mushrooms
100 g, sliced

Chicken stock
3 litres

Cream
200 g

Salt
to taste

Chicken Wanton

Wanton skin
10 pieces, chopped

Prawn meat
100 g, chopped

Chicken mince
150 g

Garlic
20 g, peeled and finely chopped

Ground white pepper
2 g

Finely sliced coriander (cilantro)
1 tsp

Finely sliced spring onions (scallions)
1 tsp

Fried shallots
1 tsp

Sesame oil
$^1/_2$ tsp

Salt
to taste

METHOD

- Melt butter in a soup pot, sauté onion, garlic, freshly crushed black peppercorn until aromatic. Add oregano, basil leaves, marjoram and all mushrooms. Sauté until fragrant.

- Pour in the chicken stock. Bring to simmer for 20 minutes.

- Pour into a food processor and blend until fine.

- Bring the mushroom soup to the boil, add cream and salt to taste.

- To prepare Chicken Wanton, mix all the wanton ingredients together well. Place 1 teaspoonful of chicken mince mixture onto a piece of wanton skin and wrap it up. Heat oil in a pan and deep-fry until golden brown.

- Stir butter into the soup before serving. Garnish with deep-fried wanton.

INGREDIENTS

Chicken mince
2 kg

Leek
20 g, diced

Celery
20 g, diced

Carrot
20 g, skinned and diced

Onion
50 g, peeled and diced

Bay leaves
2

Parsley stem
20 g

Fresh thyme
3 g

Dried basil
3 pinches

White peppercorns
1 Tbsp

Salt
1 Tbsp

Egg whites
7, reserve the egg shells

Chicken stock
5 litres

Dry sherry
10 tsp

Nyonya Chicken Money Bag
Filo pastry
10 pieces

Chives
10, blanched

Mixture A
Chicken thigh
500 g, minced

Shallots
50 g, peeled and sliced

Ginger torch bud (Bunga kantan)
1/2

Lemon grass
2 stalks, minced

Lime leaves
5, finely chopped

Bird's eye chillies
5, finely chopped

Garlic
20 g, peeled and finely chopped

Lime Kasturi
3, juiced

Salt
to taste

White pepper powder
1/3 tsp

Sugar
to taste

Garnish
Chives
10

METHOD

- Mix chicken mince, leek, celery, carrot, onion, bay leaves, parsley stem, fresh thyme, basil, peppercorns, salt, egg whites and egg shells together well.

- Add the chicken mixture to the chicken stock and stir well with a wooden spatula until the stock is cloudy.

- Heat up the stock, stirring occasionally. Do not allow the stock to boil.

- When the stock almost starts to boil, stop stirring and lower heat. Simmer until stock is reduced to half. At this time, you will notice that the chicken meat has gathered together to form a layer of patty.

- Keep aside to cool. The layer of meat will sink to the bottom of the soup pot.

- Use a medium-sized soup ladle to skim away all the excess oil from the surface of the consommé.

- Ladle the consommé onto a muslin cloth and strain through. Do not disturb or break the patty otherwise the consommé will turn cloudy.

- Combine all the ingredients of Mixture A, then place a portion on a piece of filo pastry, and tie it up with blanched chive to form like a money bag. Repeat the process until you get 10 portions.

- Heat up the oven at 180°C, bake the money bag for 20 minutes or until the meat is cooked.

- Pour the consommé into a soup plate and top with crispy money bag and garnish with a chive.

- Add a teaspoon of dry sherry into the consommé before serving.

Chicken

CONSOMMÉ
WITH NYONYA CHICKEN
MONEY BAG

INGREDIENTS

Olive oil
100 ml

Butter
50 g

Garlic
50 g, peeled and chopped

Onion
80 g, peeled and cubed

Mixed herbs in oil
1 Tbsp

Freshly crushed black peppercorns
$^2/_3$ tsp

Leek
40 g, cubed

Celery
50 g, cubed

Carrot
60 g, cubed

Broccoli
60 g, sliced

Cauliflower
60 g , sliced

French beans
100 g , sliced

Mushroom beans
100 g

Potato
150 g, cubed

Bay leaves
3

Tomato paste
80 g

Tomato
500 g, concasse

Vegetable stock
4 litres

Kuzukiri
50 g

Basil pesto sauce
50 g

Oysters
10

Garnish
Finely sliced spring onions (scallions)

Oyster

MINESTRONE WITH KUZUKIRI

METHOD

- Heat oil and butter in a soup pot, then sauté garlic, onion, mixed herbs and freshly crushed black peppercorn.

- Put in leek, celery, carrot, broccoli, cauliflower, French beans, mushroom beans, potato and bay leaves to fry until fragrant.

- Add tomato paste and tomato concasse to fry until aromatic. Later pour in the vegetable stock and bring to the boil. Simmer for 30 minutes.

- Boil water and blanch the *kuzukiri*. Remove from heat and chill in cold water. Strain.

- Stir in basil pesto sauce and *kuzukiri* before serving.

- Serve with fresh oyster and garnish with finely sliced spring onions.

Tom Yam

CAPPUCCINO WITH FRESH YABBIES

INGREDIENTS

Chicken stock
3 litres

Fresh yabbies
20

Tamarind slices
10, soaked in hot water and drained

Soy bean oil
80 ml

Onion
50 g, peeled and sliced

Lemon grass
5 stalks, smashed

Bird's eye chillies
10, smashed

***Tom Yam* paste**
200 g

Ginger torch bud (*Bunga kantan*)
1, halved

Lime leaves
10

Coriander (cilantro) stems
30 g

Lime juice
to taste

Sugar
to taste

Salt
to taste

Ground white pepper
$1/3$ tsp

Coconut cream
200 ml

Cooking cream
80 ml

Garnish
Milk foam
10 Tbsp

METHOD

- Boil the chicken stock and add the fresh yabbies to cook. Remove from heat and chill in cold water.

- Reserve the chicken stock and add tamarind slices. Bring to the boil and simmer for 10 minutes. Set aside for use later.

- Heat oil in a soup pot, sauté onion, lemon grass, chilli padi and *tom yam* paste until fragrant. Add in the prepared chicken stock, ginger flower, lime leaves and Chinese parsley stem. Fry for 5 minutes.

- Add lime juice, sugar, salt and pepper to taste. Lastly, add in the coconut cream and cooking cream. Strain the soup.

- Garnish with a spoonful of milk foam and cooked yabbies.

INGREDIENTS

Fresh strawberry fruit
75 g

Frozen strawberry fruit
75 g

Strawberry yoghurt
150 g

Strawberry ice cream
350 g

Cream
150 g

Garnish
Strawberry fruit

Fresh mint leaves

Chilled
STRAWBERRY SOUP

METHOD

- Put all the ingredients into a food processor and blend until fine. Serve chilled with fresh strawberry fruit and mint leaves.

INGREDIENTS

Egg
1, beaten

Soy bean oil
1 Tbsp

Shallots
20 g, peeled and finely sliced

Bamboo shoots
60 g, cut into fine strips

Fresh Shiitake mushroom
60 g, finely sliced

Young ginger
10 g, grated

Chicken stock
1.5 litres

Crabmeat
150 g

Chinese cooking (*Shao Hsing*) wine
3 Tbsp

Corn flour (cornstarch)
4 Tbsp

Light soy sauce
1 Tbsp

White pepper powder
1 tsp

Spring onions (scallions)
20 g, cut into fine strips

Crab sticks
2, julienned

Egg white
1

Vietnamese Lobster Spring Roll
Vietnamese rice paper
6 pieces

Cucumber
50 g, julienned

Iceberg lettuce
60 g, cut into fine strips

Carrot
40 g, julienned

Bean sprouts
30 g, blanched

Lobster meat
180 g, cooked and sliced

Mint leaves
12

Roasted almond flakes
30 g

Chinese Mayonnaise
Mayonnaise
150 g

Condensed milk
30 ml

Lemon juice
20 ml

You can enjoy the sweetness of the crabmeat and savour the crunchiness of the fresh lettuce and lobster meat in this soup.

METHOD

- Lightly beat egg with fork. Heat oil in a small omelette pan, add egg and swirl pan to coat side and base of the pan evenly. Loosen edges of egg with spatula, turn and cook the other side. Remove from pan, roll up and slice into thin strips. Set aside for use later.

- Place each sheet of rice paper individually into a bowl of warm water for about 1/2 minute or until softened. Gently lift from water and place on board.

- Cut cucumber in half lengthways, remove seeds and julienne.

- Top each sheet of rice paper with lettuce, cucumber, carrot, bean sprouts, lobster meat, mint leaves and roasted almond flakes.

- Fold bottom half of rice paper up and fold the sides inwards then roll over to enclose filling. Repeat until you get 6 portions. Keep chilled.

- For the soup, heat oil in soup pot and stir-fry shallots, bamboo shoots, mushroom and ginger until aromatic.

- Pour in the chicken stock and bring to the boil. Add crabmeat and *Shao Hsing* wine and simmer for 5 minutes. Stir in mixture of corn flour and water to thicken the soup, followed by light soy sauce, white pepper powder, spring onion and julienned crabsticks.

- Beat egg white with a little water. Add to soup in a thin stream.

- Serve the soup in a cup, accompanied with Vietnamese lobster spring roll and Chinese Mayonnaise.

Chinese

CRABMEAT SOUP

SERVED WITH VIETNAMESE
LOBSTER SPRING ROLL

Rasam

YONG TAU FOO

INDIAN SPICED SOUP
WITH DRIED CHILLI AND
FISH PASTE STUFFED
YONG TAU FOO

INGREDIENTS

Soy bean oil
80 ml

Dried chillies
5, soaked in hot water

Curry leaves
1 sprig

Garlic
8 cloves, peeled

Coriander roots
1 stalk

Cumin seeds
$1/2$ Tbsp, toasted

Coriander seeds
$1/2$ Tbsp, toasted

Lemon juice
to taste

Black peppercorns
$1/2$ Tbsp, roasted

Water
800 ml

Tamarind water
2 litres (with 800 g Tamarind paste)

Salt
to taste

***Yong Tau Foo* (4 types)**
10 portions

Onions
2, peeled and cut into wedges

Garnish
Coriander (cilantro)
30 g, finely sliced

Curry leaves

Dried chillies

METHOD

- Heat oil in soup pot, sauté dried chillies, curry leaves and garlic until fragrant. Add in the rest of the ingredients except for the *Yong Tau Foo* and onions. Bring to the boil and simmer for 30 minutes. Strain the rasam stock.

- Place the *Yong Tau Foo* and onion wedges into the rasam stock. Bring to the boil until the *Yong Tau Foo* are cooked.

- Garnish with coriander, curry leaves and dried chillies before serving.

INGREDIENTS A

Butter
100 g

Garlic
30 g, peeled and chopped

Leek
40 g, diced

Celery
50 g, diced

Carrot
50 g, skinned and diced

Onion
1, peeled and diced

Freshly crushed black peppercorns
1/2 Tbsp

Galangal
30 g, skinned and sliced

Prawn shells
500 g, cleaned and baked

Tomato paste
60 g

Chicken stock
3 litres

Saffron
1 g

INGREDIENTS B

Olive oil
50 ml

Scallops
6

Half shell mussels
6

Tiger prawns
6

Calamari
150 g, sliced

Fresh clams
100 g, cleaned

Kaffir lime leaves
7

Celery
50 g, diced

Carrot
50 g, skinned and diced

Onion
50 g, peeled and diced

Coriander (cilantro)
10 g, finely sliced

Roma tomatoes
500 g, blanched, skinned, seeded, diced

Pernod liqueur
60 ml

Salt
to taste

Puff pastry
6 pieces, enough to cover the soup cup

Egg
1, beaten for egg wash

METHOD

- Melt butter in a soup pot, sauté garlic, leek, celery, carrot, onion, freshly crushed black peppercorns and galangal until aromatic. Add in baked prawn shells and tomato paste. Stir well until fragrant.

- Pour in chicken stock and saffron. Bring to the boil and simmer for 25 minutes. Remove from heat. Pour into a food processor and blend. Strain through fine sieve.

- Heat oil in pan, sauté ingredients B and flavour with Pernod liqueur. Add to the prepared stock and bring to the boil or until the seafood is cooked. Adjust seasoning to taste.

- Pour the soup into a soup cup. Brush the puff pastry with egg wash and cover the rim.

- Place the cup in the preheated oven and bake at 180°C for 15–20 minutes or until the puff pastry turns golden brown.

Bouillabaisse

OF ATLANTIC SEAFOOD "EN CROUTE"

INGREDIENTS

Garlic
20 g, peeled and chopped

Onion
50 g, peeled and minced

Freshly crushed black peppercorns
$^1/_3$ tsp

Cumin seeds
1 tsp, roasted

Celery
30 g, minced

Pumpkin
1 kg, sliced

Potato
100 g, cubed

Chicken stock
4 litres

Dumpling skin
10 sheets

Egg
1, beaten for egg wash

Butter
80 g

Cream
200 g

XO sauce
for serving

Chinese Prawn Dumpling
Prawn meat
10 pieces

Chicken mince
200 g

Celery
20 g, diced

Carrot
20 g, skinned and diced

Salt
to taste

Ground white pepper
$^1/_4$ tsp

Garlic
20 g, finely chopped

Sesame oil
$^1/_2$ tsp

Coriander (cilantro)
15 g, finely chopped

Corn flour (cornstarch)
2 tsp

Soy bean oil
1 Tbsp

Soda bicarbonate
$^1/_3$ tsp

Water chestnut
50 g, skinned and diced

Cumin

SCENTED PUMPKIN SOUP
WITH CHINESE PRAWN DUMPLING

METHOD

- Melt butter in a pot, sauté garlic, onion, freshly crushed black peppercorns and cumin seeds until aromatic, followed by celery, pumpkin and potato.

- Add chicken stock and bring to the boil. Simmer for 20 minutes. Remove and blend until fine. Strain through a fine sieve.

- To make Chinese Prawn Dumplings, combine all the dumpling ingredients and toss well.

- Place the prawn mixture onto a sheet of dumpling skin, brush egg wash around the edge and fold it over.

- Cook the dumpling in boiling water. Remove and rest in cold water.

- Bring the soup to the boil. Stir in butter and cream before serving. Serve the soup with Chinese Prawn Dumpling and XO sauce.

INGREDIENTS

Soy bean oil
80 ml

Garlic
20 g, peeled and finely chopped

Leek
40 g

Winter melon
500 g, sliced

Chinese cooking (*Shao Hsing*) wine
50 ml

Sesame oil
$1/3$ Tbsp

Chicken stock
2 litres

Salt
to taste

Ground white pepper
2 pinches

Processed shark's fin
120 g

Winter
MELON SOUP WITH SHARK'S FIN

METHOD

- Heat oil in wok, stir-fry garlic and leek until aromatic then add in winter melon to fry for 5 minutes.

- Add Chinese cooking wine and sesame oil to fry. Pour in the chicken stock.

- Bring to the boil and simmer until the winter melon is tender.

- Remove from heat, pour into a food processor and blend until fine. Add salt and pepper to taste.

- Top with shark's fin before serving.

Hot and Sour

SZE CHUAN SOUP WITH SALMON SASHIMI

INGREDIENTS

Cooking oil
60 ml

Shallots
30 g, peeled and finely chopped

Garlic
20 g, peeled and finely chopped

Chilli bean paste
2 Tbsp

Red chilli
30 g, finely chopped

Chicken stock
2 litres

Shanghai vegetables
60 g, washed and sliced into fine strips

Bamboo shoots
60 g, washed and sliced into fine strips

Chinese cooking (*Shao Hsing*) wine
1 Tbsp

Soy sauce
3 Tbsp

Vinegar
3 Tbsp

Sesame oil
1 tsp

Salt
to taste

Pepper
to taste

Corn flour (cornstarch)
as required

Bean curd, soft
80 g, sliced into strips

Egg white
1, beaten

Chicken thigh
60 g, deboned and sliced into fine strips

Turkey ham
60 g, sliced into fine strips

Shiitake mushrooms
50 g, sliced

Norwegian salmon fillet
270 g, sliced

Chilli oil
2 Tbsp

METHOD

- Heat oil in wok, stir-fry shallots, garlic, chilli bean paste and chilli until fragrant. Pour in the chicken stock, Shanghai vegetables and bamboo shoots and bring to the boil.

- Adjust seasoning with Chinese cooking wine, soy sauce, vinegar, sesame oil, salt and pepper.

- Bring to the boil and thicken with corn flour. Remove from heat.

- Add in the sliced soft bean curd, egg white, chicken strips, turkey ham and mushroom slices. Stir well.

- Serve the soup topped with slices of Norwegian salmon and chilli oil.

ENTRÉE

asian

twist

Fresh Tiger prawns
480 g, peeled and with tails left on

Salt
$1/4$ tsp

White pepper
$1/4$ tsp

Butter
300 g

Garlic
60 g, peeled and finely chopped

Freshly crushed black peppercorns
$1/2$ tsp

Red chilli
25 g, finely chopped

Mixed herbs in oil
20 g

White wine (Riesling wine is recommended)
4 Tbsp

Salt
to taste

Herb and Garlic Toast Rings
French loaf
1

Garlic herb oil
20 ml

Garnish
Fresh basil leaves

Deep-fried *kuzukiri*

Garlic

TIGER PRAWNS

SAUTÉED WITH CHILLI
AND PROVENÇALE
HERBS IN A GARLIC
BUTTER SAUCE

METHOD

- Season the prawns with salt and pepper.

- Melt butter in pan, sauté garlic, freshly crushed black peppercorns, red chilli and mixed herbs until fragrant.

- Add prawns to fry. Deglaze with white wine.

- Adjust seasoning with salt.

- To make Herb and Garlic Toast Rings, slice the french loaf diagonally and brush with garlic herb oil. Roll it to form a ring. Bake lightly until crispy. Make 4 portions.

- Fill up the toast ring with the garlic tiger prawn and garnish with fresh basil leaf and deep-fried *kuzukiri*.

INGREDIENTS

Butter
50 g

Garlic
10 g, peeled and finely chopped

Freshly crushed black peppercorns
$1/4$ tsp

Australian asparagus
480 g, trimmed and halved

Salt
to taste

Parmesan cheese
40 g, grated

Salmon roe (*Ikura*)
2 Tbsp

Spicy Orange Foam
Orange juice
100 ml

Milk
100 ml

Cooking cream
100 ml

Orange cordial
to taste

Tabasco sauce
3 drops

Lemon juice
2 Tbsp

Sugar
$1/2$ tsp

METHOD

Melt butter in pan, sauté garlic and freshly crushed black peppercorns until fragrant.

- Add asparagus to fry until tender. Add salt to taste. Remove.

- To make Spicy Orange Foam, reduce the fresh orange juice to half then pour into the fresh milk and cooking cream. Bring to the boil. Add orange cordial, Tabasco sauce, lemon juice and sugar to taste.

- Arrange the asparagus on a serving plate and sprinkle with some grated Parmesan cheese. Gratinate under a salamander or bake in a preheated oven until golden brown.

- Whisk the orange sauce to create foam and lace over the asparagus.

- Serve the salmon roe on top of the asparagus.

Asparagus

PARMIGIANA

INGREDIENTS

Cod fish fillet
320 g, diced

Lemon
$1/2$, juiced

Salt
$1/4$ tsp

White peppercorn
$1/4$ tsp, ground

Fresh basil leaves
3, finely chopped

Coriander (cilantro)
5 g, finely chopped

Olive oil
$1 1/2$ Tbsp

Water chestnuts
50 g, skinned and diced

Hollandaise sauce
4 Tbsp

Cherry tomatoes
2

Honey-Shoyu Reduction
Cooking oil
1 Tbsp

Shallot
1, peeled and sliced

Indonesian dark soy sauce (*Kicap manis*)
150 ml

Honey
90 ml

Kalamansi juice
to taste

Sugar
to taste

Wasabi Ebico Oil
Olive oil
4 Tbsp

Wasabi ebico
$1/2$ Tbsp

Salt
to taste

METHOD

- Marinate the cod fish with lemon juice, salt and pepper.

- Add fresh basil leaves, coriander, olive oil and water chestnuts. Toss well. Keep chilled for use later.

- For the Honey-*Shoyu* Reduction, heat oil in pan and sauté shallot until fragrant. Then add the Indonesian dark soy sauce and honey. Bring to the boil and simmer until reduced to half. Add kalamansi juice and sugar to taste.

- For *Wasabi Ebico* Oil, mix all the ingredients and set aside for use later.

- To serve, fill a round cutter with the marinated codfish. Press firmly and remove the cutter. Repeat the process until you have 4 portions.

- Pour the prepared Hollandaise sauce over the cod fish parfait, and gratinate under a salamander until golden brown.

- Serve with *Wasabi Ebico* Oil and Honey-*Shoyu* Reduction.

Marinated

COD FISH PARFAIT

GRATINATED WITH
HOLLANDAISE SAUCE
AND WASABI EBICO OIL

Baked

TRIO OYSTER

WITH CRABMEAT, POTATO AND CASHEW NUT SAMOSA

INGREDIENTS

Oysters
12

Parmesan cheese
50 g, grated

Japanese mayonnaise
4 tsp

Hollandaise sauce
4 tsp

Tom Yam Dressing
Mayonnaise
200 g

***Tom Yam* paste**
25 g

Hot water
30 ml

Lemon juice
25 ml

Coriander (cilantro)
5 g, finely sliced

Spring onion (scallion)
5 g, finely sliced

Sugar
20 g

Plum sauce
15 g

Crispy Samosas
Soy bean oil
50 ml

Shallots
20 g, peeled and finely chopped

Garlic
10 g, peeled and finely chopped

Curry leaves
5

Potato
200 g, diced

Crabmeat
120 g

Curry powder
$1/2$ Tbsp

Coriander powder
$1/2$ tsp

Chicken stock
1 cup

Spring roll skin
8

Cashew nuts
40 g, roasted and crushed

Garnish
Truffle

Avocado Salsa (refer to pg 38)
4 tsp

Coriander (cilantro)

METHOD

- Clean oysters and top with grated Parmesan cheese. Place under salamander to gratinate until golden brown.

- To make Crispy Samosas, heat oil in pan, sauté shallots, garlic and curry leaves until aromatic. Add potato, crabmeat, curry powder and coriander powder to fry. Pour in the chicken stock to simmer until potato is cooked. Remove from heat.

- Cut a piece of spring roll skin into a 5 x 15-cm rectangle. Place the filling and cashew nuts at the edge, fold one end over the other side to enclose filling and create a triangular shape. Continue the process until done.

- Heat oil in pot and deep-fry samosas until golden brown. Remove from heat and place on a piece of kitchen towel to absorb the excess oil.

- Serve the oysters with 3 different toppings; Mayonnaise, Hollandaise sauce and *Tom Yam* Dressing. Garnish with truffles, Avocado Salsa and coriander, accompanied with crispy samosas.

INGREDIENTS

Butter
50 g

Garlic
10 g, peeled and finely chopped

Paprika
a pinch

Tiger prawns
12, shelled with tails left intact

Green peas
300 g, sautéed with butter and mashed

Russet potato
50 g, boiled and mashed

Cooking cream
50 ml

Butter
25 g

Salt
to taste

Freshly crushed black peppercorns
a pinch

Grapes and Walnut Sauce
Olive oil
1 Tbsp

Shallots
2, peeled and finely sliced

Freshly crushed black peppercorns
¼ tsp

Green grapes
12, skinned and seeded, halved

Walnuts
30 g, roasted

White wine
200 ml

Fish stock reduction
200 ml

Salt
to taste

Sugar
to taste

METHOD

- Combine butter, garlic and paprika. Rub over the Tiger prawns.

- Melt butter in pan, pan-fry Tiger prawns until done. Keep warm.

- Put the green pea and Russet potato mash in a pot, add cream and butter. Heat up and stir well. Add salt and freshly crushed black peppercorns to taste.

- To make Grapes and Walnut Sauce, heat olive oil in pan, sauté shallots and freshly crushed black peppercorns until aromatic. Add grapes and walnuts to fry.

- Deglaze with white wine and pour in the fish stock reduction. Simmer for 2 minutes or until you get the consistency of the sauce.

- Adjust seasoning with salt and sugar.

- Place the green pea mash on a serving plate and top with Tiger prawns. Serve it with Grapes and Walnut Sauce.

Pan-seared
TIGER PRAWNS
ON WARM GREEN PEA MASH

Pan-seared

DUCK BREAST

SERVED WITH APPLE AND BEAN CURD ROULADE

Duck breast
200 g

INGREDIENTS A

Chinese cooking (*Shao Hsing*) wine
50 ml

Garlic
10 g, peeled and crushed

***Sze Chuan* pepper**
1 g

Star anises
2

Onion
1/3, peeled and cut into wedges

Young ginger
15 g, skinned and sliced

Light soy sauce
60 ml

Salt
to taste

Sugar
to taste

Apple and Bean Curd Roulade
Lettuce
4 portions

Green apple
1, julienned

Mint leaves
5, chopped

Coriander (cilantro)
3 g, finely chopped

Japanese bean curd
100 g, cubed

Avocado
50 g, ripe, cubed

Almond flakes
1 tsp, roasted

Chinese mayonnaise
100 g

METHOD

- Trim the duck breast and place into a salad bowl. Combine all Ingredients A and pour over duck breast to marinate overnight.

- For Apple and Bean Curd Roulade, blanch lettuce and drain. Toss the rest of the ingredients together well and place on blanched lettuce. Roll up lettuce firmly like a spring roll. Repeat until ingredients are used up. Keep chilled.

- Heat oil in pan, lightly pan-sear the marinated duck breast until medium done. Keep warm.

- To serve, slice the duck breast and place over Apple and Bean Curd Roulade.

SCALLOP GRATINEE
WITH CHAR-GRILLED
PORTABELLO MUSHROOM
AND PERNOD SCENTED
HERB CREAM SAUCE

INGREDIENTS

US scallops
160 g

Butter
30 g

Garlic
10 g, peeled and finely chopped

Onion
10 g, peeled and finely chopped

Mixed herbs in oil
10 g

Freshly crushed black peppercorns
a pinch

Pernod liqueur
50 ml

Fish stock
100 ml

Cooking cream
200 ml

Salt
to taste

Portabello mushrooms
4, peeled and trimmed

Cayenne pepper
1/4 tsp

Paprika
1/4 tsp

Balsamic vinegar
1 Tbsp

Salt
to taste

Freshly crushed black peppercorns
2 pinches

Olive oil
60 ml

Grated Parmesan cheese
4 tsp

Garnish
Red radish
cut into sticks

Boiled asparagus

METHOD

- Pan-sear scallops with butter. Remove, set aside.
- Melt butter in pan, sauté garlic, onion, mixed herbs and freshly crushed black peppercorn until fragrant. Add scallop and flambé with Pernod liqueur.
- Pour in prepared fish stock and cooking cream. Bring to the boil and season.
- Season the Portabello mushrooms with cayenne pepper, paprika, Balsamic vinegar, salt, freshly crushed black peppercorn and drizzle with olive oil. Char-grill until done.
- Place the char-grilled Portabello mushroom on a plate, then top with scallop and sauce.
- Sprinkle Parmesan cheese over the scallop and gratinate under a salamander until golden brown.
- Garnish with red radish and boiled asparagus.

Steamed

BEAN CURD
WITH KAFFIR LEAF CHICKEN RAGU

Ragu is an Italian dish which is a hearty meat in tomato stew normally served with pasta. In this recipe, I add the kaffir leaf in the ragu and serve warm with steamed soft bean curd, making a very light and tasty dish.

INGREDIENTS

Soft bean curd (*tofu*), white
2 packets

Garlic oil
30 ml

Olive oil
80 ml

Garlic
30 g, peeled and finely chopped

Onion
15 g, peeled and finely chopped

Leek
10 g, finely chopped

Celery
10 g

Carrot
10 g, skinned and finely chopped

Freshly crushed black peppercorns
1 tsp

Chicken mince
250 g

Kaffir lime leaves
5, finely chopped

Fresh basil leaves
3, finely sliced

Lemon grass
2 stalks, chopped

Tomato paste
25 g

Roma tomatoes
300 g, chopped

Chicken stock
100 ml

Tomato ketchup
50 g

Salt
to taste

Pepper
to taste

Garnish
Thinly sliced lemon grass

METHOD

- Remove the bean curd from packet and use a round cutter to cut. Place it on a baking tray then drizzle with garlic oil. Steam for 10 minutes.

- Heat olive oil in same pot, sauté garlic, onion, leek, celery, carrot and freshly crushed black peppercorn until fragrant.

- Add chicken mince and fry until done. Later, add Kaffir lime leaves, basil leaves and lemon grass. Followed by tomato paste, chopped Roma tomatoes and chicken stock. Stir well and simmer for 10 minutes or until the chicken mince is tender.

- Add tomato ketchup, salt and pepper to taste.

- Pour the chicken ragu over the steamed bean curd and garnish with thinly sliced lemon grass.

Veal

CAMPAGNOLA
WITH SAUTÉED WILD MUSHROOM, BABY SPINACH AND MELTED FONTINA CHEESE

INGREDIENTS

Veal tenderloin
480 g, cut into 40 g slices

Paprika
3 pinches

Salt
2 pinches

Freshly crushed black peppercorn
3 pinches

Butter
50 g

Garlic
30 g, peeled and chopped

Onion
30 g, peeled and sliced

Baby spinach
300 g

Salt
to taste

Fontina cheese
120 g, sliced

Pasta sauce (refer to pg 157)
200 g

Garnish
Butter
50 g

Garlic
5 g, peeled and chopped

Shiitake mushroom
50 g, sliced

Sun-dried tomato
30 g, sliced

Spring onions
10 g, finely sliced

METHOD

- Season veal with paprika, salt and freshly crushed black peppercorn. Pan-fry until medium done. Set aside.

- Melt butter in pan, sauté garlic and onion until fragrant. Add baby spinach to fry and add salt to taste. Remove from heat.

- Place a piece of veal escalope on a plate and top with sautéed spinach. Repeat for the second piece of veal.

- Place the sliced Fontina cheese over the third piece of veal and bake in the preheated oven at 180°C for 10 minutes until the cheese melts.

- Melt butter and sauté garlic and Shiitake mushrooms. Serve with pasta sauce and garnish with sautéed Shiitake mushrooms, sun-dried tomato and sliced spring onions.

INGREDIENTS

Sea bass fillet
350 g, skinned, thinly sliced

Honeydew melon
160 g, cut into 12 rectangular pieces

Tobiko
50 g

Lemon zest
10 g

Frisee
50 g

Warm *Hoisin* Dressing
Corn oil
50 ml

Balsamic vinegar
25 ml

***Hoisin* sauce**
45 g

Onion
7.5 g, peeled and finely chopped

Coriander leaf
2.5 g, finely chopped

Ginger
2 g, skinned and finely chopped

Sugar
5 g

Five-spice powder
a pinch

Lime juice
to taste

METHOD

- Arrange sea bass fillets on honeydew melon.

- Sprinkle *tobiko*, lemon zest and frisee over the fish.

- To make Warm *Hoisin* Dressing, combine all the dressing ingredients and slightly heat up the dressing with medium heat to about 60–70°C then serve.

Sea Bass

MILLE-FEUILLE

WITH HONEYDEW MELON AND A WARM
HOISIN DRESSING

Chicken

SATAY CHEE CHEONG FUN AND FRIED SHALLOT OIL

INGREDIENTS

Shallots
30 g, peeled

Garlic
25 g, peeled

Ginger
20 g, skinned

Lemon grass
3 stalks

Fresh turmeric
25 g, skinned

Galangal
20 g, skinned

Chicken thigh
500 g, deboned and cut into strips

Brown sugar
2 Tbsp

Salt
1/3 tsp

Spicy peanut sauce
180 g

Chee Cheong Fun
4 rolls

Cabbage round
150 g, finely sliced

Cucumber
150 g, julienned

Red chillies
25 g, sliced

Romaine lettuce
4 pieces

Fried shallot oil
100 ml

Shoyu dressing
Higashimaru Shoyu
25 ml

Mitsukan Suehiro Su (vinegar)
50 ml

Mirin
100 ml

***Bonito* flakes**
5 g

Garnish
Sesame seeds
1 tsp

Fried shallots
30 g

METHOD

- Combine shallots, garlic, ginger, lemon grass, fresh turmeric and galangal. Put into a food processor and blend with a bit of water until fine.

- Mix well with the chicken meat, add brown sugar and salt. Marinate for 3 hours.

- Heat up the pan, sauté the marinated satay chicken meat until done. Toss well with spicy peanut sauce. Remove.

- For *Shoyu* Dressing, mix all the dressing ingredients together and keep chilled for 1 hour. Strain.

- Steam the *Chee Cheong Fun* roll then open out into a sheet slowly.

- Place the cooked satay chicken meat in the middle with some crunchy cabbage, cucumber, red chillies and Romaine lettuce. Roll it up firmly and slice into 4 portions. Arrange it on a serving plate and drizzle with fried shallot oil.

- Garnish with sesame seeds and fried shallots and serve with warm *Shoyu* Dressing.

FISH & SEAFOOD

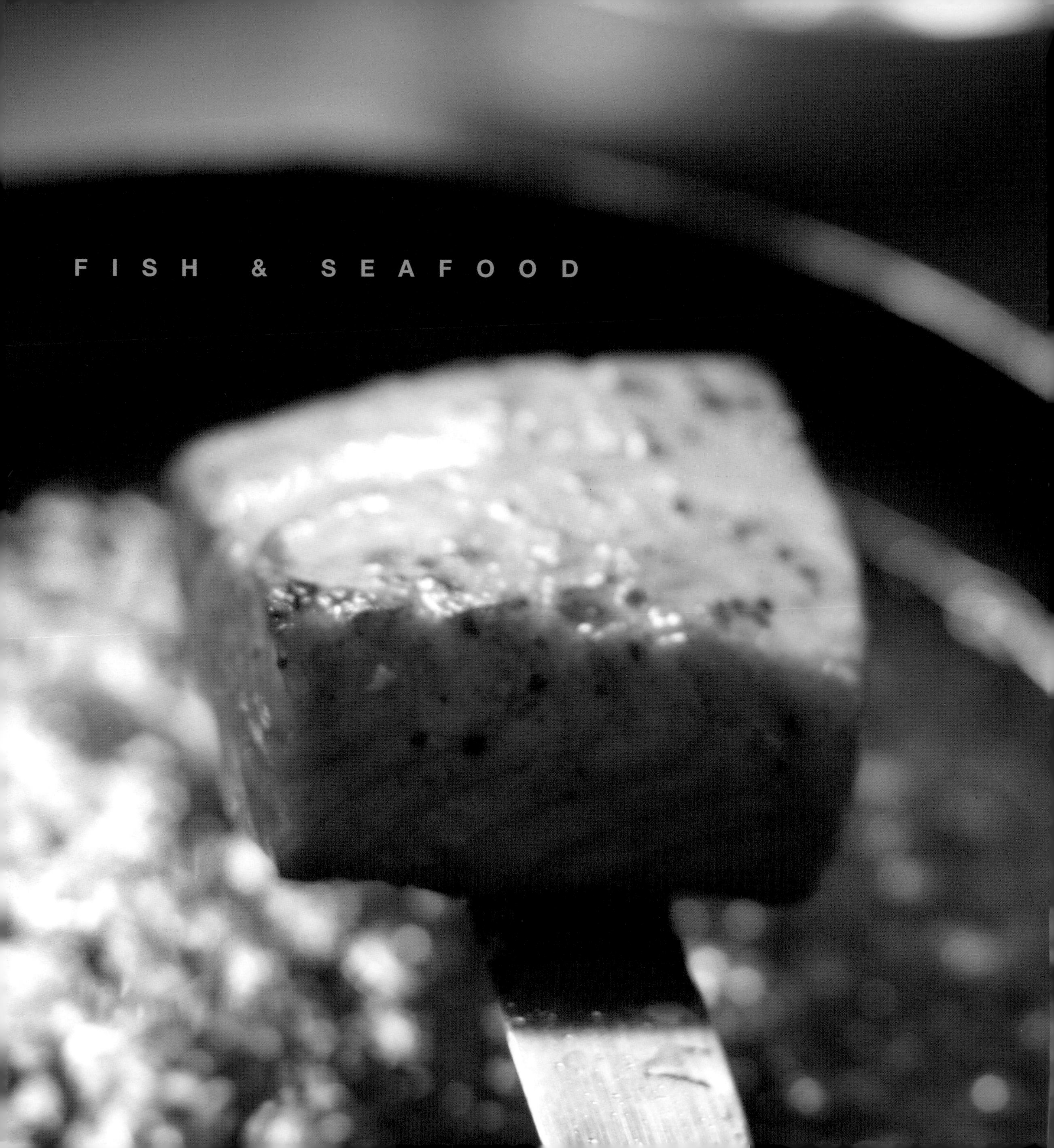

asian

twist

Roast

**STEAMED FILLET OF
BLACK COD**

INGREDIENTS

Soy bean crumb
1 piece

Soy bean oil
300 ml

Black cod fillet
640 g

Salt
3 pinches

Ground white pepper
2 pinches

Wasabi Mashed Potato
Russet potato
350 g, boiled, peeled, mashed

Cream
80 ml

***Wasabi* paste**
20 g

Salt
to taste

Pepper
to taste

Butter
30 g

Kicap Manis-Kalamansi Sauce
Cooking oil
2 Tbsp

Shallots
2, peeled and sliced

Galangal
20 g, skinned and grated

Lemon grass
2 stalks, grated

Indonesian dark soy sauce (*Kicap manis*)
300 ml

Chicken jus
180 ml

Sugar
to taste

Kalamansi juice
2–3 Tbsp

Vegetables
Garlic
20 g, peeled and chopped

Butter
30 g

Hong Kong baby Chinese kale (*kai lan*)
240 g, blanched

Salt
to taste

Garnish
Carrot
skinned and julienned

Spring onion (scallion)
julienned

Red chilli
julienned

Coriander (cilantro)

METHOD

- For soy bean crumbs, finely chop the soy bean crumb and heat oil in pan. Lightly fry the crumbs until golden brown. Remove from heat.

- For *Wasabi* Mashed Potato, combine all ingredients except for salt, pepper and butter, and heat up with low fire. Add salt and pepper to taste. Stir in butter before serving.

- For *Kicap Manis*-Calamansi Sauce, heat oil in pan, sauté shallots, galangal and lemon grass until fragrant. Then add in the Indonesian dark soy sauce and chicken jus, bring to the boil and simmer until reduced to half. Add sugar and calamansi juice to taste.

- Season the cod fish with salt and pepper. Steam the cod fish for 3 minutes then remove. Later roast the cod fish in the preheated oven at 180°C for another 4 minutes, depending on the thickness of the fish.

- To prepare vegetables, sauté garlic with butter, add baby Chinese kale and stir-fry for 1–2 minutes. Add salt to taste.

- To serve, place the *Wasabi* Mashed Potato in the middle of a plate and top with sautéed vegetables, cod fish and soy bean crumbs. Drizzle with *Kicap Manis*-Kalamansi Sauce. Garnish with a mixture of julienned carrot, spring onion, red chilli and coriander.

INGREDIENTS

Butter
50 g

Garlic
20 g, peeled and chopped

Mixed herbs in oil
2 tsp

Freshly crushed black peppercorns
2 pinches

Scallops
320 g

Pernod liqueur
50 ml

Cream
100 ml

Salt
to taste

Mesclun mix salad
4 portions

Homemade Bean Curd Cake
Japanese box bean curd
1 box

Japanese egg bean curd
2

Fish paste
100 g

Fresh soy bean milk
1 litre

Egg whites
2, mixed with 80 g of potato starch

Potato starch
80 g

Dried shrimp
20 g, chopped

Water chestnuts
40 g, skinned and chopped

Coriander (cilantro)
5 g

Salt
to taste

Balsamic-Ginger Butter
Butter
120 g

Ginger
20 g, skinned and grated

Balsamic vinegar
100 ml

Salt
to taste

Pepper
a pinch

METHOD

- Melt butter in pan, sauté garlic, mixed herbs and freshly crushed black peppercorns until fragrant. Add scallops and flambé with Pernod liqueur.

- Add cream to reduce and salt to taste.

- For Homemade Bean Curd Cake, place both types of bean curd, fish paste and soy bean milk into a food processor and blend until fine. Add egg white and potato starch mixture. Blend until well combined. Remove and place in a salad bowl.

- Stir in the rest of the ingredients and toss well. Pour the bean curd mixture into a tray lined with a layer of cling film. Spread it evenly and steam until done.

- Cut the bean curd cake into the desired shape and dash with potato starch. Deep-fry until golden brown.

- For Balsamic-Ginger Butter, melt 80 g of the butter in a pan, then add grated ginger and balsamic vinegar. Bring to the boil, simmer until reduced to half. Stir in the remainder of the butter and adjust seasoning with salt and pepper.

- Place the crispy Homemade Bean Curd Cake in the middle of a plate. Arrange the scallop over it and followed by a portion of mesclun mix.

- Drizzle with Balsamic-Ginger Butter around the plate.

Pan-seared

QUEEN SCALLOPS

WITH HOMEMADE BEAN CURD CAKE
AND BALSAMIC-GINGER BUTTER

Confit OF TASMANIAN SALMON

INGREDIENTS

Miso **paste**
50 g

Mirin **(rice wine)**
100 ml

Sake
50 ml

Thai chilli flakes
1/2 tsp

Sugar
to taste

Tasmanian salmon fillet
480 g

Olive oil
1 litre

Ramen
300 g, cooked

Salt
to taste

Freshly crushed black peppercorns
to taste

Olive oil
1 Tbsp

Avocado Foam
Avocado
1/2, mashed

Cream
50 ml

Fresh milk
200 ml

Lemon juice
to taste

Salt
to taste

METHOD

- Combine *miso* paste, *mirin*, *sake* and chilli flakes well. Add sugar to taste.

- Pour over the salmon fillet and marinate for 3–4 hours. Keep chilled.

- For Avocado Foam, combine all the foam ingredients and bring to the boil. Whisk until foam is formed.

- Heat 1 litre olive oil in pan, sauté *ramen* and season to taste.

- Pan-sear the salmon. In a pot, heat 1 Tbsp olive oil to 120°C. Place the salmon fillet into the hot oil and cook until medium done. Remove from oil and drain.

- To serve, drizzle the salmon fillet with Avocado Foam.

SCALLOPS
WITH SPICY KAFFIR LIME-GARLIC SAUCE

Wok-fried

Dried Shiitake mushrooms
240 g, steamed and decoratively cut

Boiling water
1 litre

Garlic
50 g, peeled and finely chopped

Chicken stock
500 ml

Soy bean oil
50 ml

Garlic
35 g, peeled and chopped

Ginger
20 g, skinned and grated

Kaffir lime leaves
5, finely chopped

Chinese chilli bean (*tau pan*) paste
1 Tbsp

Thai chilli sauce
200 g

Chicken stock
200 ml

Corn flour (cornstarch) mixture
as required

Salt
to taste

Pepper
to taste

Scallops
12, cleaned and sliced transversely

**Hong Kong baby Chinese kale
(*kai lan*)**
240 g, blanched and halved
lengthwise

Garnish
Roasted sesame seeds

Coriander (cilantro)

METHOD

- Combine the dried Shiitake mushrooms and boiling water. Set aside to soak for 3 hours. Strain through a sieve. Wok-fry the mushrooms with garlic and season to taste. Add chicken stock and simmer for 15 minutes. Strain and keep warm.

- Heat oil in wok, add garlic, ginger and kaffir lime leaves to fry until aromatic. Add the chilli bean paste and Thai chilli sauce and stir. Pour in the chicken stock, bring to the boil and slowly stir in the corn flour mixture to thicken. Add salt and pepper to taste then remove from heat.

- Heat oil in wok, lightly wok-fry the scallops.

- To serve, pour the sauce onto a plate and arrange the baby Chinese kale on it. Arrange the mushrooms and scallops in a row over the kale.

- Garnish with roasted sesame seeds and coriander.

INGREDIENTS

Chilean bass fillet
480 g, sliced into 2

Salt
2 pinches

Potato starch
100 g

Olive oil
30 ml

White *Buna Shimeiji* mushrooms
120 g

Freshly crushed black peppercorns
a pinch

Olive oil
50 ml

Salt
to taste

Green peas
350 g, boiled and mashed

Cooking cream
50 ml

Salt
2 pinches

Butter
10 g

Ginger-*Shoyu* Sauce
***Dashi* water**
310 ml

Usukuchi
50 ml

Mirin
50 ml

Hondashi
to taste

Grated ginger
1/2 tsp

Garnish
French loaf
1

Garlic herb oil

Mesclun mix salad
4 portions

METHOD

- Season the chilean bass with some salt and dash with potato starch. Heat oil in pan, lightly pan-fry the fish until done.

- Char-grill the mushrooms then sprinkle some freshly crushed black peppercorns, olive oil and salt. Combine prepared green pea mash and cream. Stir well over low heat, add salt to taste and melt butter before serving.

- For the Ginger-*Shoyu* Sauce, combine all the sauce ingredients and bring to the boil. Remove and keep warm.

- Slice the French loaf diagonally, brush the slice with garlic herb oil and roll it to form a ring. Bake lightly until crispy. Make 4 portions.

- To serve, place the chilean sea bass over the charred *Buna Shimeiji* mushrooms. Serve with the sauce and green pea mash, accompanied with mesclun mixed salad and herb crisps.

Pan-fried

CHILEAN BASS

SERVED WITH WHITE BUNA SHIMEIJI MUSHROOM AND GREEN PEA MASH

INGREDIENTS

Swordfish (*Mekajiki*) fillets
4 (120 g each)

Salt
3 pinches

Pepper
2 pinches

Onion
20 g, peeled and cubed

Garlic
5 g, peeled and chopped

Butter
30 g

Celery
10 g, cubed

Corn kernel
10 g

**Green vegetable soy beans
(Edamame)**
20 g

Water chestnut
20 g, skinned and cubed

Sun-dried tomato
60 g, cubed

Carrot
10 g, skinned and cubed

Shiitake mushrooms
100 g, cubed

***Shimeiji* mushrooms**
100 g

Barley
25 g, cooked

Coriander (cilantro)
5 g, finely sliced

White wine
50 ml

Fish stock
200 ml

Salt
to taste

Pepper
to taste

Fermented Soy Bean (*Taucu*) Butter
Sauce
Butter
200 g

Shallots
20 g, peeled and sliced

Fermented soy beans (*taucu*)
40 g, ground

***Hoisin* sauce**
20 g

Pepper
to taste

Sugar
to taste

Fish stock
80 ml

Lemon juice
to taste

Green Tabasco Emulsion
Cream
100 ml

Fresh milk
150 ml

Green Tabasco
as required

Salt
to taste

Sugar
to taste

Garnish
Red radish
4 portions, julienned

Chives
8

METHOD

- Place the *Mekajiki* fillet on a rectangular tray, sprinkle with salt and pepper. Pan-sear on preheated pan until done.

- For Fermented Soy Bean Butter Sauce, melt one-third of the butter and sauté the shallots. Add ground fermented soy beans, *Hoisin* sauce, pepper, sugar and fish stock. Reduce and add lemon juice to taste. Remove from heat and strain through a fine sieve. Stir in two-thirds of butter before serving.

- For the risotto, sweat the onion and garlic with butter, then add the rest of the ingredients except for white wine, fish stock, salt and pepper. Sauté until fragrant, deglaze with white wine and fish stock. Simmer for 2–3 minutes. Add salt and pepper to taste.

- For Green Tabasco Emulsion, mix all the ingredients and bring to the boil. Use a whisk to whip until foamy.

- To serve, place the fish on a serving plate and drizzle with Fermented Soy Bean Butter Sauce and Green Tabasco Emulsion. Garnish with julienned red radish and chives.

Oven-roasted

MEKAJIKI

SERVED WITH MUSHROOM AND SUN-DRIED TOMATO RISOTTO, FERMENTED SOY BEAN BUTTER SAUCE AND GREEN TABASCO EMULSION

Baked
CRAB WITH MILK, HERBS AND ROMAINE LETTUCE

INGREDIENTS

Soy bean oil
80 ml

Crabs
4 (200 g each), halved

Chinese cooking (*Shao Hsing*) wine
50 ml

Chicken stock
1 litre

Evaporated milk
250 ml

Polygonum (*laksa*) leaves
3 stalks

Ginger
30 g, skinned and sliced

Lemon grass
2 stalks, smashed

Bird's eye chillies, whole
8

Salted vegetables
60 g, washed and sliced

Salt
to taste

Sugar
to taste

***Laksa* noodles**
240 g

Romaine lettuce
200 g

Garnish
Ginger
julienned

Coriander (cilantro)

Garlic oil

METHOD

- Heat oil in wok. Add crabs and fry. Add in Chinese cooking wine and fry for 2 minutes. Remove from heat.

- Combine chicken stock, evaporated milk, polygonum leaves, ginger, lemon grass and bird's eye chillies. Bring to the boil and simmer until aromatic.

- Place the salted vegetables and crab in the stock. Bring to the boil. Add salt and sugar to taste.

- To serve, place a crab into a soup bowl, with blanched *Laksa* noodles and crispy Romaine lettuce underneath. Pour the soup over and garnish with julienned ginger and coriander. Drizzle with garlic oil before serving.

INGREDIENTS

Snapper fillets
480 g

Salt
to taste

Pepper
to taste

Olive oil
30 ml

Garlic
20 g, peeled and sliced

Onion
30 g, peeled and sliced

Baby spinach
300 g, sautéed

Gingko nuts
30 g

Prepared crispy kataifi ring
4

Sesame Spice Crust

Fennel seeds
10 g, toasted

Cumin seeds
10 g, toasted

Thai red chilli flakes
1 g

Sesame seeds
10 g, roasted

Garlic
10 g, peeled and chopped

Orange zest
10 g

Lemon zest
10 g

Freshly crushed black peppercorns
2 pinches

Curry leaves
1 tsp, deep-fried and crumbled

Mango-Curry Sauce

Butter
30 g

Shallots
10 g, peeled and sliced

Green apple
40 g, peeled and cubed

Banana
30 g, peeled and sliced

Curry powder
1 Tbsp

Fish stock
400 ml

Mango chutney
1 Tbsp

Turmeric powder
$1/4$ tsp

Cream
4 Tbsp

Salt
to taste

Pepper
to taste

Sugar
to taste

Lemon juice
to taste

METHOD

- For Sesame Spice Crust, mix all the ingredients together well. Set aside.

- Season the fish. Lightly pan-sear and top with Sesame Spice Crust. Roast in a preheated oven at 180°C for 5–7 minutes or until done.

- For Mango-Curry Sauce, melt butter in pan, sauté shallots until fragrant. Add the green apple, banana and curry powder to fry for 2–3 minutes.

- Pour in the fish stock. Bring to the boil and reduce to half. Strain through a fine sieve.

- Stir in mango chutney, turmeric powder and cream. Add salt, pepper, sugar and lemon juice to taste.

- Heat olive oil and fry garlic and onion until aromatic. Sauté baby spinach and gingko nuts.

- To serve, fill the crispy kataifi ring with sautéed baby spinach and gingko nuts. Serve the fish with Mango-Curry Sauce.

Open-fire

ROASTED SESAME SPICED CRUSTED SNAPPER FILLET

INGREDIENTS

Butter
30 g

Turkey ham
80 g, julienned

Freshly crushed black peppercorns
to taste

Sauerkraut
120 g

Water chestnuts
50 g

Ricotta cheese
40 g, cubed

Spring roll skin
4

Egg
1, beaten

Soy bean oil (for deep-frying)
1 litre

Red spotted Garoupa fillet
480 g

Salt
to taste

Pepper
to taste

Garlic
10 g, peeled and chopped

Pea sprouts
150 g

Salt
to taste

Pepper
to taste

Kung Pao Sauce
Soy bean oil
15 ml

Onion
15 g, peeled and sliced

Ginger
10 g, skinned and grated

Dried chilli
6 g, soaked in water then drained

Chinese cooking (*Shao Hsing*) wine
1 Tbsp

Oyster sauce
20 g

***Hoisin* Sauce**
20 g

Chicken stock
500 ml

Soy sauce
15 ml

Corn flour (cornstarch)
as required

Sesame oil
1 tsp

Salt
to taste

Pepper
to taste

Sugar
to taste

Garnish
Crispy knishes

Avocado Salsa (refer to pg 38)

METHOD

- Melt butter in pan and sauté turkey ham and freshly crushed black peppercorns until aromatic. Add in sauerkraut and water chestnuts. Remove from heat, let it cool down then toss with Ricotta cheese.

- To make crispy knishes, place the sauerkraut mixture onto a piece of spring roll skin and roll it up tightly. Seal the edge with beaten egg. Repeat the process until done.

- Heat oil in pan, deep-fry the knishes until golden brown then remove from heat.

- Place garoupa fillet on a tray and season with salt and pepper. Pan-sear the fish and bake in the preheated oven at 180°C for 6–8 minutes.

- Heat oil in pan and sauté garlic until aromatic. Add pea sprouts to fry and add salt and pepper to taste.

- For *Kung Pao* Sauce, sauté onion, ginger and dried chilli until fragrant. Add the rest of the ingredients except corn flour and bring to the boil. Simmer for 2 minutes. Thicken the sauce with corn flour.

- To serve, place the pea sprouts on a serving plate followed by the garoupa fillet. Accompany with crispy knishes, Avocado Salsa and *Kung Pao* Sauce.

Pan-seared
RED SPOTTED GAROUPA
WITH SAUERKRAUT, HAM AND WATER CHESTNUT
KNISH IN A CLASSICAL KUNG PAO SAUCE

Wok-fried

ATLANTIC SEAFOOD
WITH CRISPY YUBA IN GINGER-EGG SAUCE

INGREDIENTS

Soy bean oil
100 ml

Garlic
10 g, peeled and chopped

Freshly crushed black peppercorns
a pinch

Curry leaves
1 stalk

Ocean seafood (scallop, mussel, Tiger prawn and red garoupa)
400 g

Lily bulb, fresh
30 g

Shimeiji **mushrooms**
50 g

Chinese cooking (*Shao Hsing*) wine
3 Tbsp

Salt
to taste

Ohban yuba
4 pieces, deep-fried

Ginger-Egg Sauce
Soy bean oil
500 ml

Egg whites
2, beaten

Salted black bean
1 tsp

Chicken stock reduction
350 ml

Ginger
20 g, skinned and grated

Salt
to taste

METHOD

- For the Ginger-Egg Sauce, heat soy bean oil in wok to 70–80°C, pour the beaten egg whites through a conical sieve into the oil. Lightly stir until cooked and floating on the surface of the oil. Strain and set aside for use.

- Wash the salted black bean with water then drain. Re-use the oil and bring to 160–180°C. Lightly deep-fry the black bean. Remove from heat.

- Bring the chicken stock reduction to the boil, add in grated ginger and the prepared egg white. Add salt to taste. Stir in black bean before serving.

- To serve, heat oil in wok, fry the garlic, freshly crushed black peppercorns and curry leaves until fragrant, then add the seafood, lily bulb and *Shimeiji* mushrooms to fry. Deglaze with Chinese cooking wine and add salt to taste.

- Pour the Ginger-Egg Sauce onto the plate to cover the surface of the plate. Then place the crispy *yuba* and top with mixed seafood.

Cajun

SPICE SEA BASS

SERVED WITH A MISO-ORANGE
LEMON GRASS SAUCE

INGREDIENTS

Sea bass fillets
480 g

Cajun spice seasoning
1 Tbsp

Corn flour (cornstarch)
300 g

Soy bean oil (for deep-fat frying)
1 litre

Baby French beans
240 g

Garlic
5 g, peeled and chopped

Dried scallops
10 g, deep-fried

Salt
to taste

Pepper
to taste

Miso Orange-Lemon Grass Sauce
White wine
70 ml

Orange juice
250 ml

Lemon grass
1 stalk, smashed

White *miso* paste
1 tsp

Cream
80 ml

Orange cordial
to taste

Lemon juice
to taste

Sugar
to taste

Egg yolk
1

Butter
50 g

Garnish
Kuzukiri
4 portions, deep-fried

METHOD

- Season the sea bass fillets with Cajun spice seasoning for 3 hours. Use a sharp knife to make a diagonal incision, in opposite directions on the fillet without cutting through the fish.

- Dash both sides of fish with corn flour.

- Heat oil in wok, deep-fry the fish until crispy and golden brown. Remove and place on kitchen tissues to absorb excess oil.

- Re-use the oil to blanch the baby French beans. Strain and then stir-fry with some garlic and crispy dried scallops. Season to taste. Place the French beans into a round ring, press firmly and then remove the ring. Garnish with crispy *kuzukiri*.

- For the *Miso* Orange-Lemon Grass Sauce, mix white wine, orange juice and lemon grass together. Bring to the boil and simmer to reduce until half. Strain through a fine sieve.

- Add miso paste, cream, orange cordial, lemon juice and sugar to taste. Stir in egg yolk and butter before serving.

Pan-seared
YELLOW TAIL TUNA
SERVED WITH MANGO AND ASPARAGUS PARMIGIANA WITH A SPICY SZE CHUAN SAUCE

INGREDIENTS

Butter
30 g

Garlic
10 g, peeled and chopped

White asparagus
16, trimmed

Grated Parmesan cheese
4 Tbsp

Yellow tail tuna
400 g

Spicy *Sze Chuan* Sauce
Shallots
30 g, peeled

Garlic
20 g, peeled

Pickled leek
30 g

Red chilli
50 g

Bird's eye chilli
5 g

Soy bean oil
2 Tbsp

Fermented soy beans (*taucu*)
30 g, crushed

Chilli *bo*
50 g

Sour plum sauce
20 g

Sugar
to taste

Salt
to taste

Chicken stock
400 ml

Garnish
Mango
120 g, peeled and cubed

METHOD

- For Spicy *Sze Chuan* Sauce, finely chop shallots, garlic, pickled leek, red chilli and chilli padi. Heat oil in wok and stir-fry until fragrant.

- Add fermented soy beans, chilli *bo* and plum sauce. Stir well. Add sugar and salt to taste. Add chicken stock if the sauce is too thick or dry.

- Melt butter in pan and sauté garlic and asparagus. Remove from heat and place on a serving plate. Sprinkle with grated Parmesan cheese and gratinate under a salamander until golden brown or until the Parmesan cheese melts.

- Lightly pan-sear the tuna. Slice into pieces and arrange over the asparagus and garnish with mango cubes.

- Serve with the Spicy *Sze Chuan* Sauce.

Char-grilled

TIGER PRAWNS
WITH THAI HOLLANDAISE SAUCE

INGREDIENTS A

Tiger prawns
16, cleaned and deveined

Salt
to taste

Freshly crushed black peppercorns
1 tsp

Chopped garlic
1 Tbsp

Honey
50 g

Chinese rose wine
60 ml

Soy bean oil
3 Tbsp

Plain sushi rolls
4 portions

Sesame seeds
30 g, roasted

Thai Hollandaise Sauce
Egg yolks
3

Clarified butter
300 g

Japanese rice wine vinegar
1 Tbsp

Kaffir lime leaves
2, finely chopped

Finely chopped torch ginger bud
(*Bunga kantan*)
1 tsp

Bird's eye chillies
2, finely chopped

Finely chopped lemon grass
1/2 tsp

Finely chopped coriander (cilantro)
10 g

Salt
to taste

Sugar
to taste

METHOD

- For Thai Hollandaise Sauce, place a round stainless steel bowl on top of a bain-marie. Add the egg yolks and stir in the clarified butter with a whisk until done.

- Add the vinegar and the rest of the ingredients. Stir well until a sauce is formed and keep warm.

- Season the prawns with some salt, freshly crushed black peppercorns and garlic. Mix honey with Chinese rose wine and soy bean oil then set aside for use later.

- Char-grill Tiger prawns, basting with the honey mixture until done.

- Shell the prawns, leaving tails intact. Place the prawns over the plain sushi rolls coated with roasted sesame seeds. Serve with Thai Hollandaise Sauce.

Siamese
GREEN CURRY LAKSA

Soy bean oil
50 ml

Baby aubergine (brinjal)
60 g

Lemon grass
2 stalks

Kaffir lime leaves
5

Thai green curry paste
100 g

Chicken stock
1 litre

Polygonum (*laksa*) leaves
2 stalks

Bean curd puffs (*tau fu pok*)
4, halved

Fresh coconut milk
200 ml

Fish sauce
to taste

Sugar
to taste

***Soba* noodles**
400 g

Garnish
**Fresh assorted sashimi
(*Toro*, butter fish and salmon)**
240 g, sliced

Bean sprouts
80 g

Cucumber
80 g, julienned

Mint leaves
4 sprigs

METHOD

- Heat oil in pot, sauté aubergine, lemon grass and kaffir lime leaves until fragrant. Add Thai green curry paste to fry.

- Pour in chicken stock and polygonum leaves. Bring to the boil and simmer for 5–10 minutes.

- Add bean curd puffs and fresh coconut milk. Stir well. Add fish sauce and sugar to taste.

- To serve, blanch the *soba* noodles and place in a bowl. Pour in the Siamese curry *laksa* broth and garnish with sliced sashimi, bean sprouts, cucumber and mint leaves.

MEAT & POULTRY

asian
twist

Lemon-lime
CHILLI OSSOBUCCO

130

INGREDIENTS

Veal shank
4 (250 g each), cut into 2.5-cm thickness

Salt
2 pinches

Pepper
a pinch

Corn flour (cornstarch)
100 g

Sauce
Soy bean oil
50 ml

Garlic
10 g, peeled and chopped

Onion
20 g, peeled and diced

Carrot
15 g, skinned and diced

Dried chillies
2, soaked in water, drained

Lemon grass
2 stalks, finely chopped

Galangal
15 g, skinned

Torch ginger bud (*Bunga kantan*)
$1/2$, finely chopped

Tomato paste
30 g

Roma tomatoes
600 g, chopped

Beef stock
1 litre

Beef brown sauce
250 ml

Kaffir lime leaves
5

Salt
to taste

Sugar
to taste

Risotto
Butter
50 g

Garlic
10 g, peeled and chopped

Freshly crushed black peppercorns
2 pinches

Shiitake mushrooms
80 g, sliced

Arborio rice
160 g

Chinese cooking (*Shao Hsing*) wine
50 ml

Chicken *kut teh* broth
500 ml

Grated Parmesan cheese
4 Tbsp

Salt
to taste

Garnish
Leek
julienned

METHOD

- Season the veal shank, dust with flour, shallow-fry the veal shank until golden brown. Remove from heat.

- Heat oil in deep-frying pan. Sauté garlic, onion, carrot, dried chillies, lemon grass, galangal and torch ginger bud until aromatic. Then add in tomato paste to fry for 5–10 minutes followed by chopped Roma tomatoes, beef stock, beef brown sauce and kaffir lime leaves. Bring to the boil and put in the veal shank. Simmer until the meat is tender.

- Add salt and sugar to taste.

- For Risotto, heat butter in pan. Sauté garlic and freshly crushed black peppercorns until aromatic. Add Shiitake mushrooms followed by Arborio rice. Fry for 2 minutes and deglaze with Chinese cooking wine. Pour in the chicken *kut teh* broth and bring to the boil. Simmer until the rice is cooked. Remove from heat and add in the grated Parmesan. Stir until well combined. Add salt to taste.

- To serve, pour the sauce on a dinner plate and then followed by Risotto and braised veal shank. Garnish with julienned leek.

INGREDIENTS

Chicken breast fillets
4 (160 g each)

Salt
2 pinches

Freshly crushed black peppercorns
2 pinches

Paprika
1 tsp

Mushroom Duxelles
Butter
50 g

Garlic
10 g, peeled and chopped

Onion
15 g, peeled and diced

Mixed herbs in oil
2 tsp

Freshly crushed black peppercorns
2 pinches

Shiitake mushrooms
300 g, diced

White wine (optional)
50 ml

Salt
to taste

Gorgonzola blue cheese
80 g, cubed

Tomato, Roasted Shallot and Grappa Coulis
Olive oil
2 Tbsp

Garlic
2, peeled and chopped

Shallots
30 g, whole, roasted

Freshly crushed black peppercorns
2 pinches

Grappa
20 ml

Tomato sauce
300 ml

Salt
to taste

Sculpted Vegetables
Baby courgettes (zucchini)
4

Lotus roots
4

New potatoes
4

Saffron
a few threads

Tomatoes
4

Olive oil
80 ml

Lemon
1/2, juiced

Salt
to taste

Pepper
to taste

METHOD

- For Mushroom Duxelles, melt butter in pan, sauté garlic, onion, mixed herbs and freshly crushed black peppercorns until aromatic. Add Shiitake mushrooms to fry for 2 minutes. Deglaze with white wine and add salt to taste. Remove from heat and set aside for use later.

- Clean and butterfly the chicken breast without breaking into 2 pieces. Season with salt, freshly crushed black peppercorns and paprika. Place the mushroom duxelles in the middle of the chicken breast and top with Gorgonzola blue cheese. Fold up the bottom of the chicken breast and roll it up like a spring roll. Tie it tightly with butcher string. Repeat process for the remaining chicken breasts. Set aside.

- For Tomato, Roasted Shallot and Grappa Coulis, heat oil in saucepan, sauté garlic, roasted shallots and freshly crushed black peppercorns until fragrant. Flambé with grappa and add tomato sauce. Simmer for 5–10 minutes. Pour into food processor and blend until fine. Add salt to taste.

- Lightly pan-fry the stuffed chicken roulade and bake in the preheated oven at 180°C for 25 minutes or until done.

- Trim the courgettes and lotus roots. Cook each separately in salt water. Peel the potatoes and boil in salt water, adding saffron towards the end to colour. Cut the tomatoes into cylinders.

- To serve, untie the chicken roulade and cut into thick slices. Serve with sculpted vegetables drizzled with a mixture of olive oil, lemon juice, salt and pepper. Serve hot with Tomato, Roasted Shallot and Grappa Coulis.

Stuffed

CHICKEN ROULADE

WITH GORGONZOLA CHEESE AND MUSHROOM DUXELLES, TOMATO, ROASTED SHALLOT AND GRAPPA COULIS

INGREDIENTS

Lamb rack
4 portions (380 g each), cut into 3 pieces

Salt
to taste

Pepper
to taste

Paprika
1 tsp

Macadamia-Coconut Crust
Macadamia nuts
100 g, roasted, crushed

Coconut flesh
80 g, freshly grated and toasted

Honey
60 g

Garlic
5 g, peeled and chopped

Fresh thyme
2 stalks, finely chopped

Parsley
5 g, chopped

Asian Ratatouille
Soy bean oil
2 Tbsp

Garlic
15 g, peeled and chopped

Onion
25 g, peeled and chopped

Ginger
5 g, skinned and grated

Carrot
25 g, skinned and cubed

Aubergine (brinjal)
20 g, cubed

Green and red capsicum
20 g, cubed

Gingko nuts
20 g

French beans
20 g, cubed

Water chestnuts
15 g, cubed

Oyster sauce
to taste

Light soy sauce
to taste

Sesame oil
to taste

Tomato
50 g, concasse

Coriander (cilantro)
1 tsp, chopped

Lobster Basmati Pilaf
Butter
50 g

Onion
20 g, peeled and diced

Bay leaf
1

Freshly crushed black peppercorns
2 pinches

Basmati rice
150 g

Chicken stock
250 ml

Lobster meat
100 g, cooked and diced

Mint leaf
1 tsp, finely chopped

Red chilli
1, chopped

Cashew nuts
30 g, roasted, crushed

Salt
to taste

Rosemary Infused Lamb Jus
Lamb jus
400 ml

Fresh rosemary
1 tsp, chopped

Madeira wine
2 Tbsp

Shallots
2, peeled and sliced

Freshly crushed black peppercorns
a pinch

Salt
to taste

METHOD

- Sauté the Asian Ratatouille ingredients and keep warm for later.

- For Macadamia-Coconut Crust, combine all the ingredients and mix well. Set aside.

- For Rosemary Infused Lamb Jus, mix all the ingredients except for salt, bring to the boil and simmer for 2–3 minutes. Strain and add salt to taste.

- To cook the Lobster Basmati Pilaf, melt butter and sauté onion, bay leaf and freshly crushed black peppercorns until fragrant. Add in basmati rice to fry. Later pour in the chicken stock, stir well and cook until done.

- Once the rice is cooked, add the cooked lobster meat, chopped mint, red chilli and cashew nuts. Add salt to taste, toss well and keep warm.

- Season lamb with salt, pepper abd paprika. Pan-sear the lamb and spread the top with Macadamia-Coconut Crust. Put into the preheated oven at 180°C and bake for 15 minutes or until medium done.

- Serve with Asian Ratatouille, Lobster Basmati Pilaf and Rosemary Infused Lamb Jus.

Macadamia-

COCONUT ENCRUSTED RACK OF LAMB,

LOBSTER BASMATI PILAF AND ROSEMARY INFUSED LAMB JUS

INGREDIENTS

Chicken drumsticks
4 (250 g each)

Corn flour (cornstarch)
60 g

Butter
50 g

Garlic
10 g, peeled and chopped

Onion
20 g, peeled and chopped

Tomato paste
40 g

Mixed herbs in oil
1 Tbsp

Freshly crushed black peppercorns
a pinch

Mushrooms (Abalone/Shiitake/Oyster)
120 g

Pickled onions
5

Black olives
3, sliced

Green stuffed olives
3, sliced

Capers
1 tsp

Lemon
$1/3$, zest grated

Tomatoes
1 kg, peeled and chopped

Chicken stock
300 ml

Wok-fried Black Pepper *Udon*
Soy bean oil
2 Tbsp

Onion
30 g, peeled and sliced

Freshly crushed black peppercorns
5 g

Asparagus
50 g

Nama Udon
350 g, blanched

Oyster sauce
1 tsp

Salt
to taste

Sugar
to taste

Garnish
Iceberg lettuce
julienned

Dried bean curd sticks (*fu chok*)
deep-fried

METHOD

- Season the chicken and coat with corn flour. Deep-fry until half done, remove from oil and drain.

- Melt butter in pot, sauté garlic, onion, tomato paste, mixed herbs and freshly crushed black peppercorns until fragrant. Add mushrooms, pickled onion, black olives, green olives, capers and lemon zest to fry for 2 minutes.

- Pour in the chopped tomatoes, chicken stock and chicken drumsticks. Stir well, bring to the boil and simmer until done.

- For Wok-fried Black Pepper *Udon*, heat oil in wok, stir-fry onion and freshly crushed black peppercorns until aromatic. Add asparagus, *udon* and oyster sauce to fry. Add salt and sugar to taste.

- Garnish the chicken with julienned iceberg lettuce and deep-fried dried bean curd sticks.

Chicken

CACCIATORE

SERVED WITH
WOK-FRIED
BLACK PEPPER
UDON

INGREDIENTS

Beef mince
600 g

Garlic
15 g, peeled and chopped

Coriander (cilantro)
15 g, chopped

Red chilli
15 g, chopped

Green chilli
15 g, chopped

Kaffir lime leaves
6

Fried shallots
3 Tbsp

Whole egg
1

Sesame oil
1 tsp

Salt and pepper
to taste

Corn flour (cornstarch)
15 g

Shallots
20 g, peeled and sliced

Thai red curry paste
120 g

Fresh coconut milk
200 ml

Chicken stock
800 ml

Polygonum (*laksa*) leaves
2 stalks

Longans (canned)
50 g, drained

Asparagus
120 g

Fish sauce
to taste

Sugar
to taste

Garlic Fried Rice
Soy bean oil
2 Tbsp

Garlic
50 g, peeled and chopped

Carrot
20 g, skinned and chopped

Cooked white rice
400 g

Soy sauce
1 Tbsp

Pepper
2 pinches

Fish sauce
to taste

Thai

RED CURRY MEAT BALLS WITH LONGAN AND ASPARAGUS
SERVED WITH GARLIC FRIED RICE

METHOD

- For meat balls, toss well beef mince, garlic, coriander, red and green chilli, kaffir lime leaves, fried shallots, whole egg, sesame oil, salt and pepper. Add a little bit of corn flour.

- Divide the mixture into 20 meat balls. Set aside.

- Heat oil in pot, sauté shallots and Thai red curry paste until aromatic. Add meat balls and fry for 5 minutes, then pour in fresh coconut milk, chicken stock and *laksa* leaves. Stir well and simmer until the meat balls are cooked.

- Add longans, asparagus, fish sauce and sugar to taste. Keep warm.

- For Garlic Fried Rice, heat oil in wok, stir-fry garlic and carrot until fragrant. Add the cooked rice and soy sauce to fry. Add pepper and fish sauce to taste.

Tandoori

OSTRICH FILLET

WITH APPLE AND MELON SALAD

INGREDIENTS

Ostrich fillet
400 g

***Tandoori Marinade**
80 g

Plain yoghurt
80 ml

Red food colouring
as required

Apple and Melon Salad

Green apple
1, cut into small matchsticks

Honeydew melon
60 g, cut into small matchsticks

Rock melon
60 g, cut into small matchsticks

Mint leaf
1 sprig, finely sliced

Lemon
1/2, juiced

Sugar
to taste

Lemon Grass Fried Rice

Soy bean oil
2 Tbsp

Lemon grass
2 stalks, finely chopped

Garlic
5 g, peeled and chopped

Shallots
20 g, peeled and sliced

Dried shrimps
30 g

Cooked white rice
400 g

Fried egg omelette
1, shredded

Spring onions (scallions)
1 Tbsp, finely sliced

Fish sauce
to taste

Pepper
2 pinches

Sugar
to taste

*Tandoori Marinade
Ginger
20 g, skinned and grated

Garlic
15 g, peeled and ground

Chilli powder
15 g

Meat curry powder
15 g

Garam masala
10 g

Cumin powder
10 g

Ground coriander
10 g

Freshly crushed black peppercorns
2 g

Lime juice
to taste

Salt
to taste

METHOD

- For Tandoori Marinade, toss all the ingredients and rub over the ostrich fillet together with plain yoghurt and red food colouring. Marinate for 3–4 minutes.

- For Apple and Melon Salad, toss all the ingredients and keep chilled.

- For Lemon Grass Fried Rice, heat oil in wok, stir-fry lemon grass, garlic, shallots and dried shrimps until fragrant then add cooked rice and shredded egg omelette. Stir well with spring onions and season with fish sauce, pepper and sugar.

- Pan-sear the tandoori ostrich fillet and bake in a preheated oven at 180°C for 15 minutes or until medium done.

- Slice the tandoori ostrich fillet and serve with Apple and Melon Salad and Lemon Grass Fried Rice.

INGREDIENTS

Lamb leg
4 portions (150 g each), deboned and cubed

Ginger
60 g, skinned and grated

Sesame oil
30 g

Coriander leaves
6 g, chopped

Sesame seeds
8 g, roasted

Freshly crushed black peppercorns
5 g

Garlic
15 g, peeled and chopped

Soy sauce
30 ml

Sugar
to taste

Pineapple
100 g, skinned and cubed

Leek
60 g, sliced

Capsicums
60 g, cut into squares

Thai Cherry Tomato Salad

Cherry tomatoes
400 g, halved

Shallots
80 g, peeled and thinly sliced

Kaffir lime leaves
10, deep-fried until crispy and then crumbled

Lime juice
to taste

Olive oil
80 ml

Salt
to taste

Freshly crushed black peppercorns
a pinch

Mongolian Chilli Sauce

Chilli *bo*
100 g

Sesame oil
1 g

Garlic oil
1 g

Grated ginger
2 g

Green capsicum
10 g, chopped

Spring onion (scallion)
10 g, finely sliced

Coriander leaf
5 g, chopped

Garlic
1 clove, peeled and chopped

Fish sauce
to taste

Sugar
to taste

Sesame seed
1 g

METHOD

- Marinate lamb cubes with grated ginger, sesame oil, coriander leaves, sesame seeds, freshly crushed black peppercorns, garlic, soy sauce and sugar to taste for 6 hours.
- For Thai Cherry Tomato Salad, combine all the salad ingredients and toss well. Keep chilled for use later.
- For Mongolian Chilli Sauce, mix all the sauce ingredients and keep chilled for use later.
- Use a bamboo stick to skewer the marinated lamb cubes together with pineapple cubes, leek and capsicums. Repeat until all the lamb cubes are used up.
- Grill the kebabs on a char-broil until done. Serve with Thai Cherry Tomato Salad and Mongolian Chilli Sauce.

PASTA

asian

twist

Spinach,

MACADAMIA AND RICOTTA CAPPELLACCI

INGREDIENTS

Spinach
300 g

Onion
1, peeled and sliced

Butter
50 g

Fresh basil leaf
2 g, finely sliced

Macadamia nuts
50 g, roasted, chopped

Salt and pepper
to taste

Ricotta cheese
100 g

Pasta dough*
200 g

***Pasta Dough (makes 1 kg)**
Wheat flour
1 kg

Whole eggs
10

Salt
10 g

Olive oil
25 ml

Garlic Butter Sauce
Butter
150 g

Garlic
30 g, peeled

Mixed herbs in oil
1 tsp

Freshly crushed black peppercorns
a pinch

Cream
60 ml

Egg yolk
1

Salt and sugar
to taste

Garnish
Chervil

Frisee

METHOD

- Sweat the spinach and onion with butter then add the basil and roasted macadamia nuts. Season to taste. Remove from heat to cool.

- Toss well with Ricotta cheese.

- To make Pasta Dough, combine all dough ingredients in a mixer and knead well. Rest the dough for 1 hour. Roll a strip of pasta dough into 45–50 cm in length then cut into squares. Using a teaspoon, put a little mound of the filling in the center of each square.

- Brush a little water around the edge of each square. Fold it into half over the filling. Press the seal. Turn up the edges so that it looks like a little hat.

- For Garlic Butter Sauce, melt butter in pan, sauté garlic, mixed herbs and freshly crushed black peppercorns until fragrant. Stir in the cream and egg yolk. Add salt and sugar to taste.

- To serve, boil the Cappellacci until done. Drain and place in a pasta bowl.

- Pour the Garlic Butter Sauce over the Cappellacci and garnish with chervil and frisee.

INGREDIENTS

Olive oil
80 ml

Garlic
60 g, peeled and sliced

Hot red chillies
30 g, sliced

Chicken meat
240 g, sliced

Chinese cooking (*Shao Hsing*) wine
80 ml

Fusilli
480 g, cooked until al dente

Kung Pao Sauce
Cooking oil
30 ml

Onion
30 g, peeled and sliced

Ginger
15 g, skinned and sliced

Dried chillies
30 g, soaked in water, drained and halved

Chinese cooking (*Shao Hsing*) wine
30 ml

Oyster sauce
40 g

***Hoisin* sauce**
25 g

Chicken stock
500 ml

Light soy sauce
30 ml

Sesame oil
1 tsp

Salt
to taste

Pepper
to taste

Sugar
to taste

Corn flour (cornstarch)
as required

Garnish
Cashew nuts
60 g, roasted and crushed

Spring onions (scallions)
20 g, finely chopped

METHOD

- For *Kung Pao* Sauce, sauté onion, ginger and dried chillies until fragrant.

- Add the rest of the sauce ingredients. Bring to the boil. Simmer for 5–10 minutes. Add salt, pepper and sugar to taste. Thicken with corn flour.

- Heat olive oil in pan, sauté garlic and red chillies until fragrant. Add chicken meat to fry and deglaze with Chinese cooking wine.

- Add cooked fusilli and *Kung Pao* Sauce to fry.

- Garnish with roasted cashew nuts and spring onions.

Kung Pao
FUSILLI

INGREDIENTS

Tiger prawns
300 g, shelled with tails intact

Salt
2 pinches

Pepper
2 pinches

Olive oil
50 ml

Garlic
40 g, peeled and sliced

Curry leaves
3 g

Spaghetti
640 g, cooked until al dente

Bean sprouts
120 g

Red chillies
2, julienned

*Sambal Sauce
Soy bean oil
60 ml

Garlic
20 g, peeled and chopped

Red onion
40 g, peeled and sliced

Curry leaves
2 g

Prepared *sambal tumis*
150 g

Pasta sauce (refer to pg 157)
400 g

Tamarind water (50 g paste + 100 ml water)
100 ml

Salt
to taste

Sugar
to taste

Garnish
Coriander (cilantro)

METHOD

- To make *Sambal* Sauce, heat oil in a medium pot, sauté garlic, onion and curry leaves until fragrant. Add *sambal tumis* and pasta sauce. Bring to the boil.

- Add tamarind juice, salt and sugar to taste. Keep warm for use later.

- Season Tiger prawns with salt and pepper.

- Heat oil in pan, sauté garlic and curry leaves until fragrant. Add Tiger prawns to fry for 5 minutes.

- Blanch the spaghetti and place onto the pan with *Sambal* Sauce. Stir well.

- Add in bean sprouts and julienned red chilli to fry for 1 minute.

- Serve the *sambal* spaghetti on a glass plate and garnish with Chinese parsley.

Sambal
SPAGHETTI WITH TIGER PRAWNS

INGREDIENTS

Lasagna sheets
12 pieces

Bechamel sauce
300 g

Mozzarella cheese
200 g, shredded

Parmesan cheese
60 g, grated

Pasta sauce (refer to pg 157)
240 g

Beef mince
400 g

Soy bean oil
50 ml

Garlic
20 g, peeled and chopped

Shallots
30 g, peeled and sliced

Freshly crushed black peppercorns
2 pinches

Turmeric leaf
1, finely chopped

***Rendang* paste**
80 g

Lemon grass
2 stalks, sliced

Roma tomatoes
500 g, chopped

Beef stock
100 ml

Salt
to taste

Sugar
to taste

Garnish
Pine nuts
roasted

Leek
julienned and deep-fried

Beef

RENDANG LASAGNA

METHOD

- For the Beef *Rendang* Ragout, place the beef mince into a preheated non-stick pan and sauté until cooked. Remove from pan and keep for use later.

- Heat oil in pot, sauté garlic, shallots and freshly crushed black peppercorns until aromatic.

- Add the cooked beef mince, turmeric leaf, *rendang* paste and lemon grass, followed by chopped Roma tomatoes and beef stock. Add salt and sugar to taste. Keep warm.

- To make lasagna, boil the lasagna sheets then place on a baking dish.

- Spoon Beef *Rendang* Ragout onto the lasagna, top with bechamel sauce and grated Mozzarella cheese. Repeat the step until ingredients are used up.

- Sprinkle Parmesan cheese on top and bake in the preheated oven at 180°C until the cheese melts and turns golden brown. Serve with rich pasta sauce and garnish with roasted pine nuts and deep-fried julienned leek.

Olive oil
80 ml

Garlic
100 g, peeled and sliced

Dried chillies
30 g, soaked in water, drained and halved

Freshly crushed black peppercorns
2 g

Trenette
720 g, cooked until al dente

Sun-dried tomato
80 g, sliced

Salt
to taste

Garnish
Basil leaves
4

Trenette

AGLIO E OLIO

METHOD

- Heat oil in pan, sauté garlic, dried chillies and freshly crushed black peppercorn until fragrant.

- Place trenette into the pan. Stir well and add in sun-dried tomato. Add salt to taste.

- Garnish with basil leaf.

INGREDIENTS

Olive oil
60 ml

Garlic
30 g, peeled and chopped

Freshly crushed black peppercorns
2 pinches

Mixed herbs in oil
1 Tbsp

**Mixed seafood
(fish fillet, Tiger prawn, squid, mussel,scallop)**
320 g

Abalone mushrooms
100 g, sliced

Pernod liqueur
2 Tbsp

Linguine
480 g, cooked until al dente

Pasta sauce (refer to pg 157)
600 g

Salt
to taste

Parmesan cheese
40 g, shaved

Iceberg lettuce
60 g, julienned

Linguine
MARINARA

METHOD

- Heat oil in pan, sauté garlic, freshly crushed black peppercorns and mixed herbs until aromatic. Add seafood and mushrooms to fry then flambé with Pernod liqueur.

- Add linguine and pasta sauce, stir-fry for 2–3 minutes.

- Add salt to taste and garnish with shaved Parmesan cheese and julienned Iceberg lettuce.

PASTA SAUCE

MAKES 1 KG

INGREDIENTS

Olive oil
60 ml

Onion
80 g, peeled and chopped

Garlic
50 g, peeled and chopped

Freshly crushed black peppercorns
1 tsp

Tomato paste
50 g

French basil leaf
10 g, finely sliced

Dried oregano
$^1/_3$ tsp

Dried tarragon
$^1/_3$ tsp

Dried marjoram
$^1/_3$ tsp

Roma tomatoes
1 kg, peeled and chopped

Tomato ketchup
80 g

Salt
to taste

Sugar
to taste

METHOD

- Heat oil in pan, sauté onion, garlic and freshly crushed black peppercorns until fragrant. Add tomato paste and herbs and sauté for 3 minutes.

- Pour in chopped Roma tomatoes. Simmer for 5–10 minutes.

- Add tomato ketchup, salt and sugar to taste.

Spaghetti

LOBSTER

WITH GARLIC, CURRY LEAF AND EVAPORATED MILK

INGREDIENTS

Lobster
4 (300 g each), cleaned and halved

Salt
2 pinches

Freshly crushed black peppercorns
2 pinches

Butter
30 g

Garlic
20 g, peeled and chopped

Spaghetti
480 g, cooked until al dente

Olive oil
2 Tbsp

Cheese Sauce
Cooking oil
50 ml

Curry leaves
3 g

Evaporated milk
500 ml

Cheddar cheese
4 slices

Fish stock
200 ml

Salt
to taste

Sugar
to taste

METHOD

- Clean and cut the lobster. Season with salt, freshly crushed black peppercorns, butter and garlic.

- Bake in the preheated oven at 180°C for 15–20 minutes or until done.

- For Cheese Sauce, heat oil in a wok, fry the curry leaves until fragrant then add evaporated milk, Cheddar cheese and fish stock. Bring to the boil and simmer for 2 minutes.

- Add salt and sugar to taste.

- Sauté spaghetti with olive oil then serve with baked lobster and creamy Cheese Sauce.

INGREDIENTS

Pasta dough (refer to pg 147)
250 g

Crabmeat Filling
Butter
50 g

Garlic
5 g, peeled and chopped

Onion
15 g, peeled and chopped

Freshly crushed black peppercorns
2 pinches

Celery
15 g, diced

Crabmeat, processed
150 g

Water chestnut
20 g, diced

Salt
to taste

Mint leaf
5 g, finely chopped

Smoked salmon
80 g, sliced

Curry Laksa Gravy
Curry *Laksa* paste
100 g

Chicken stock
400 ml

Curry leaf
1 g

Curry powder
2 tsp

Lemon grass
2 stalks

Coconut milk
80 ml

Salt
to taste

Sugar
to taste

Garnish
***Nameko* mushrooms**
char-grilled

Coriander

METHOD

- For Crabmeat Filling, melt butter in pan, sauté garlic, onion, freshly crushed black peppercorn and celery until fragrant. Add the crabmeat and water chestnut to fry and season with salt. Remove from heat to cool. Toss well with chopped mint. Set aside for use later.

- For Curry *Laksa* Gravy, combine curry *laksa* paste, chicken stock, curry leaf, curry powder and lemon grass. Bring to the boil and simmer for 5 minutes. Add coconut milk, salt and sugar to taste. Keep warm.

- To make ravioli, roll out the pasta dough and cut into 45–50-cm long strips.

- Place 5–6 little mounds of crabmeat filling and a slice of smoked salmon along one side of one of the pasta strips, spacing them out evenly.

- Using a pastry brush, carefully brush a little water onto the pasta strip around each mound of filling.

- Fold the plain side of the pasta strip over the filling. Starting from the folded edge, press down gently with your fingertips around each mound, pushing the air out at the unfolded edge. Sprinkle lightly with flour.

- With a fluted pasta wheel, cut along each long side, then inbetween each mound to make small square shapes.

- To serve, cook the ravioli in boiling water until done. Pour Curry *Laksa* Gravy over a pasta plate and top with the crabmeat and smoked salmon ravioli.

- Garnish with char-grilled *Nameko* mushrooms and coriander.

Crabmeat

AND SMOKED SALMON RAVIOLI

INGREDIENTS

Soft bean curd
160 g

Green tea *soba*
240 g, cooked

Prawn Salpicon
Butter
40 g

Garlic
10 g, peeled and chopped

Onion
10 g, peeled and chopped

Carrot
15 g, skinned and chopped

Celery
10 g, chopped

Fresh basil leaves
5 g, finely sliced

Freshly crushed black peppercorns
a pinch

Tiger prawns
300 g, diced

Pasta sauce (refer to pg 157)
300 g

Tomato ketchup
1 Tbsp

Salt
to taste

Garnish
Itogaki
10 g

Green
TEA SOBA
WITH BEAN CURD AND PRAWN SALPICON

METHOD

- For Prawn Salpicon, melt butter in pan, sauté garlic, onion, carrot, celery and basil leaves until fragrant. Add freshly crushed black peppercorns and Tiger prawns to fry.

- Pour in the pasta sauce, stir well and simmer for 3 minutes. Add tomato ketchup and salt to taste. Keep warm.

- Thinly slice the soft bean curd and place on a plate. Top with soba noodle and Prawn Salpicon.

- Garnish with *itogaki*.

Penne
IN PIQUANT CHEESE SAUCE

INGREDIENTS

Cooking cream
320 ml

Gorgonzola blue cheese
50 g

Fontina cheese
50 g

Bel Paese cheese
50 g

Butter
50 g

Asparagus
120 g, sliced

Penne rigate
600 g, cooked until al dente

Salt
to taste

Garnish
Fresh basil leaves
4

Tomato concasse
4 tsp

METHOD

- Combine cooking cream and cheese, bring to the boil and simmer to desired consistency.

- Melt butter in pan, sauté asparagus then penne rigate. Add the cheese sauce and stir well.

- Add salt to taste.

- Garnish with fresh basil leaves and tomato concasse.

Japanese

NAMA UDON AND SASHIMI

IN SPICY TOM YAM BROTH

INGREDIENTS

Nama Udon
240 g

Sashimi (Salmon, *Toro*, *Tako*)
180 g, thinly sliced

Spicy *Tom Yam* Broth
Soy bean oil
30 ml

***Tom Yam* paste**
80 g

Chicken stock
500 ml

Lemon grass
2 stalks

Bird's eye chillies
5

Kaffir lime leaves
5

Shallots
2, peeled and sliced

Coriander (cilantro)
10 g, sliced

Salt
to taste

Sugar
to taste

Vinegar
to taste

Fish sauce
to taste

Lemon Butter Sauce
Butter
100 g

Cooking cream
30 g

Lemon juice
to taste

Garnish
Seaweed
shredded

Cucumber
julienned

Sesame seeds
roasted

METHOD

- To make Spicy *Tom Yam* Broth, add all ingredients except salt, sugar, vinegar and fish sauce and bring to the boil. Simmer for 5 minutes. Add salt, sugar, vinegar and fish sauce to taste.

- Melt butter in pan and stir in cooking cream and lemon juice to make a basic Lemon Butter Sauce.

- To serve, pour in Lemon Butter Sauce into Spicy *Tom Yam* Broth. Stir well until well combined. Pour onto a plate and top with blanched *Nama Udon* and thinly sliced sashimi. Garnish with shredded seaweed, julienned cucumber and roasted sesame seeds.

PIZZA

asian
twist

INGREDIENTS

Wheat flour
1 kg, sieved

Salt
16 g

Instant yeast
50 g

Water
500 ml

Corn oil
100 ml

Pizza
DOUGH

METHOD

- In a bowl, mix the wheat flour and salt.

- Combine yeast with a little water.

- Add corn oil to the remaining water.

- Place the flour mixture into a dough mixer together with the yeast mixture. Knead at speed 1 (low speed). At the same time, pour in the oil and water mixture into the dough mixer slowly.

- Knead dough until it is not sticking any more. It should feel soft and smooth.

- Remove and place into a bowl, covered with a towel. Let dough rise for 1–2 hours or until it has doubled in volume.

PIZZA SAUCE

MAKES 1 KG

INGREDIENTS

Olive oil
60 ml

Onion
80 g, peeled and chopped

Garlic
35 g, peeled and chopped

Freshly crushed black peppercorns
1 tsp

Tomato paste
50 g

French basil leaves
10 g, finely sliced

Dried oregano
1/2 tsp

Dried tarragon
1/2 tsp

Roma tomatoes
1 kg, peeled and chopped

Tomato ketchup
60 g

Salt
to taste

Sugar
to taste

METHOD

- Heat oil in pot. Sauté onion, garlic and freshly crushed black peppercorns until fragrant. Add tomato paste and herbs then sauté for 3 minutes.

- Add chopped Roma tomatoes. Simmer for 5–10 minutes.

- Add tomato ketchup, salt and sugar to taste.

INGREDIENTS

Pizza dough (refer to pg 170)
200 g

Pizza sauce (refer to pg 171)
60 g

Mozzarella cheese
80 g, grated

Sun-dried tomato
40 g, sliced

Marinated artichokes
60 g, sliced

Black olives
2, pitted and sliced

Freshly crushed black peppercorns
2 pinches

Gorgonzola blue cheese
30 g, cubed

Sun-dried

TOMATO , ARTICHOKE AND MOZZARELLA CHEESE PIZZA

METHOD

- Roll flat the pizza dough with a rolling pin. Spread pizza sauce evenly. Sprinkle one-third of grated Mozzarella cheese.

- Top with sliced sun-dried tomato, artichokes, black olives, freshly crushed black peppercorns and Gorgonzola blue cheese.

- Lastly, sprinkle the remaining two-thirds of Mozzarella cheese over the pizza. Bake in the preheated oven at 200°C for 15 minutes.

Pizza
FRUTTI DE MARE

INGREDIENTS

Mixed seafood
120 g

Garlic
5 g, peeled and chopped

Mixed herbs in oil
10 g

Pernod liqueur
1 tsp

Salt
to taste

Pizza dough (refer to pg 170)
200 g

Pizza sauce (refer to pg 171)
60 g

Mozzarella cheese
80 g, grated

Dried oregano
a pinch

Chilli flakes
2 pinches

Provolone cheese
20 g, cubed

Garnish
Fresh chives
2 g

Macadamia nuts, roasted
30 g

Cherry tomatoes
2, cut into wedges

METHOD

- Sauté mixed seafood with garlic, mixed herbs in oil and deglaze with Pernod liqueur and add salt to taste. Remove from heat.

- Roll flat the pizza dough with a rolling pin. Spread pizza sauce evenly. Sprinkle one-third of grated Mozzarella cheese over the pizza.

- Top with sautéed seafood, oregano and chilli flakes, followed by the balance of grated Mozzarella cheese and Provolone cheese.

- Bake in preheated oven at 200°C for 15 minutes.

- Garnish with fresh chives, macadamia nuts and cherry tomatoes.

INGREDIENTS

Pizza dough (refer to pg 170)
200 g

Prepared satay sauce
80 g

Mozzarella cheese
80 g, grated

Satay chicken meat
120 g, cooked

Bombay onion
25 g, peeled and brunoise

Red chilli
20 g, sliced

Cucumber
30 g, julienned

Satay Chicken Meat Marinade
Chicken thigh
1 kg, deboned and sliced

Ginger
60 g, skinned and grated

Fresh turmeric
50 g, skinned and grated

Garlic
30 g, peeled and minced

Shallots
80 g, peeled and minced

Galangal
60 g, skinned and grated

Lemon grass
5 stalks, minced

Brown sugar
to taste

Salt
to taste

SPICY CONNECTION

METHOD

- To marinate chicken satay, combine all the ingredients and marinate for 6 hours in the refrigerator.

- Heat oil in pan, sauté the marinated chicken satay meat until done. Remove from heat and keep aside for use later.

- Roll flat the pizza dough with a rolling pin. Spread the satay sauce evenly. Sprinkle one-third of grated Mozzarella cheese over the pizza.

- Top with the cooked chicken satay meat, onion brunoise and sliced red chilli. Sprinkle the remaining Mozzarella cheese and bake in the preheated oven at 200°C for 15 minutes.

- Sprinkle with julienned cucumber over the cheesy pizza before serving.

INGREDIENTS

Pizza dough (refer to pg 170)
200 g

*Spicy Tomato Curry Sauce
60 g

Mozzarella cheese
80 g, grated

Tandoori chicken
120 g, cooked and sliced

Courgettes (zucchini)
30 g, sliced and grilled

Mango chutney
20 g

Tandoori

CHICKEN PIZZA

METHOD

- To make Spicy Tomato Curry Sauce, heat oil in pot, sauté minced shallots, garlic and ginger until fragrant. Then add in chilli powder and curry paste to fry.

- Pour in pizza sauce, coconut milk and chicken stock. Bring to the boil and simmer for 5 minutes. Add sugar, salt and pepper to taste.

- Roll flat the pizza dough, spread the top with Spicy Tomato Curry Sauce and one-third of grated Mozzarella cheese, followed by sliced Tandoori chicken meat and grilled courgettes. Finish with the remaining grated Mozzarella cheese.

- Bake at 200°C for 15 minutes. Meanwhile, prepare Tomato and Onion Salad by tossing well the onion slices, tomato and coriander with lemon juice, salt and pepper. Set aside for use later.

- Once the pizza is ready, spread some mango chutney over the pizza and sprinkle with Tomato and Onion Salad and crispy pappadom.

*Spicy Tomato Curry Sauce (500 g)

Soy bean oil
50 ml

Shallots
40 g, peeled and minced

Garlic
20 g, peeled and minced

Ginger
10 g, peeled and minced

Chilli powder
5 g

Curry paste (chicken/meat)
150 g

Pizza sauce
150 g

Coconut milk
70 g

Chicken stock
150 ml

Sugar
to taste

Salt
to taste

Pepper
to taste

Tomato and Onion Salad
Red onion
15 g, peeled and sliced

Tomato
15 g, julienned

Coriander (cilantro)
5 g, sliced

Lemon juice
to taste

Salt
to taste

Pepper
to taste

Garnish
Pappadom
20 g

INGREDIENTS

Pizza dough (refer to pg 170)
200 g

***Nyonya Sauce**
60 g

Mozzarella cheese
80 g, grated

Soft shell crabs
2

***Tempura* batter**
1 cup

Roma tomato
30 g, sliced

Bombay onion
20 g, peeled and sliced

Fried bean curd puffs (*Tau foo pok*)
20 g, sliced

Japanese mayonnaise
50 g

*Nyonya Sauce (2.5 kg)
Torch ginger bud (*Bunga kantan*)
20

Lemon grass
18 stalks

Bird's eye chillies
110 g

Assam paste
300 g, mixed with 600 ml water

Water
1.5 litres

Sugar
200 g

Salt
30 g

Lime *Kasturi*
20, juiced

Garnish
Chives

Nyonya
CRISPY SOFT SHELL CRAB PIZZA

METHOD

- To make Nyonya sauce, put torch ginger bud, lemon grass and bird's eye chillies in a food processor and blend until fine.

- Heat oil in wok, stir-fry the blended ingredients until aromatic, then pour in the assam juice and water. Bring to the boil.

- Add sugar, salt and lime *kasturi* juice to taste.

- Roll flat the pizza dough and spread Nyonya sauce over the dough evenly. Sprinkle with one-third of grated Mozzarella cheese.

- Dip the soft shell crabs into the prepared *tempura* batter and deep-fry until golden brown. Drain and cut each crab into 4 pieces. Place on the pizza dough together with sliced tomato, onion, fried bean curd puffs and the remaining grated Mozzarella cheese.

- Bake in the preheated oven at 200°C for 15 minutes. Drizzle with Japanese mayonnaise and garnish with chive before serving.

Taiwanese

SAUSAGE AND MUSHROOM PIZZA

INGREDIENTS

Pizza dough (refer to pg 170)
200 g

Pizza sauce (refer to pg 171)
60 g

***Mushroom Ragout**
100 g

Mozzarella cheese
80 g, grated

Taiwanese sausage
150 g, grilled and sliced

*Mushroom Ragout
Butter
50 g

Garlic
30 g, peeled and chopped

Onion
40 g, peeled and chopped

Mixed herbs in oil
2 Tbsp

Freshly crushed black peppercorns
2 pinches

Mixed mushrooms
400 g, sliced

Prepared chicken stock
1 Tbsp

Salt
to taste

Garnish
Sliced spring onions (scallions)
1 Tbsp

Avocado Salsa (refer to pg 38)
50 g

METHOD

- For Mushroom Ragout, melt butter in pan, sauté garlic, onion, mixed herbs and freshly crushed black peppercorns until aromatic. Add in sliced mixed mushrooms to fry. Pour in a little bit of chicken stock and add salt to taste.

- Roll flat the pizza dough, spread with pizza sauce and Mushroom Ragout evenly. Sprinkle one-third of grated Mozzarella cheese and top with sliced Taiwanese sausage.

- Finish with the remaining Mozzarella cheese.

- Bake in the preheated oven at 200°C for 15 minutes.

- Garnish with spring onions and Avocado Salsa before serving.

Seafood

TERIYAKI PIZZA

INGREDIENTS

Pizza dough (refer to pg 170)
200 g

***Teriyaki* Sauce**
60 ml

Butter
20 g

Mixed seafood
120 g, sautéed with garlic

Garlic
5 g, peeled and chopped

Salt
to taste

Mozzarella cheese
80 g, grated

Cabbage
30 g, shredded

Japanese seaweed
5 g, shredded

Japanese pickled ginger (*hajikami*)
10 g, sliced

Teriyaki Sauce (400 ml)
Mirin
160 ml

Sake
120 ml

Shoyu
160 ml

Tamari
40 ml

Sugar
to taste

Corn flour (cornstarch)
for thickening

METHOD

- For *Teriyaki* Sauce, mix all the ingredients, except sugar and cornflour, and bring to the boil. Simmer for 5–10 minutes. Add sugar to taste and thicken with cornflour.

- Roll flat the pizza dough and spread the *Teriyaki* Sauce evenly.

- Melt butter and sauté mixed seafood with garlic and add salt to taste.

- Sprinkle one-third of grated Mozzarella cheese and cooked mixed seafood on pizza dough. Finish with the remaining grated Mozzarella cheese.

- Bake the pizza in the preheated oven at 200°C for 15 minutes.

- Sprinkle the shredded cabbage, seaweed and pickled ginger over the pizza. Drizzle with *goma* dressing over the shredded cabbage before serving.

GLOSSARY

asian

twist

Bechamel sauce
A white sauce made by combining hot flavoured or seasoned milk with a roux.

Bel Paese cheese
One of Italy's best known cheeses manufactured in Lombardy made from cow's milk (45% fat content). This uncooked pressed cheese is creamy and mild. It is creamy yellow in colour, with a washed crust.

Bonito flakes
This is an important ingredient in *dashi* water. A dried *bonito* fillet looks like a 15–20-cm long brownish hunk of wood that is shaved. The flakes are often used as stock or garnish.

Concasse
The french term for chopping or pounding a substance, either coarsely or finely. For example, when skinned, seeded tomato flesh is finely chopped.

Dashi water
Japanese stock made from dried *bonito* flakes and *konbu* with soy sauce, *sake* and *miso*. It is one of the most important elements in Japanese cooking.

Enoki mushroom
This winter mushroom grows naturally worldwide. Its sticky yellow-white cap is seldom wider than 1-cm, while its long thin stalk is usually over 12.5-cm. *Enoki* mushrooms are used in soups, stews and grilled with chicken.

Fontina cheese
An Italian cow's milk cheese (45% fat content), with a pressed cooked center and brushed, sometimes oiled crust. Elastic to the touch, and with a few small holes, this cheese tastes delicately nutty.

Frisee
A bitter-tasting curly leaves salad plant originating from Asia or Egypt.

Garam masala
A blend of spices used in Indian cooking. Unlike the commercially prepared curry powder, this does not contain powdered turmeric or chilli powder.

Gorgonzola blue cheese
An Italian cow's milk cheese (48% fat content), white or light yellow and streaked with blue. Gorgonzola should be delicate and creamy with a natural grey rind, pitted with red. It has a distinct smell and can have a mellow, strong or sharp flavour, depending on its degree of maturity.

Grappa
A marc brandy made in Italy from residue of grapes left after pressing. It should ideally be matured so that the harsh initial taste is refined. Grappa is made in various regions and may be used for certain dishes, such as the Piedmontese speciality, braised kidney.

Hanaho
A type of flower used for garnishing in Japanese cooking.

Hondashi
A type of ready-made *dashi* in powder form that you can purchase in a grocery shop.

Japanese pickled ginger (Hajikami)
These pickled ginger shoots are used to garnish many Japanese meals.

Kataifi
This is an Arabic delicacy which is made from rice flour. It is mainly used for dessert or savoury dishes. It can be prepared by baking in the oven or by deep-fat frying.

Kuzukiri
An arrowroot noodle in dried form. Often used in salads, appetizers and soups.

Lamb jus
It is primarily used for the gravy of a roast lamb, made by diluting the pan juices with water, clear stock or the goodness in the pan that has been absorbed into the stock.

Marjoram
Native to the Mediterranean area, the leaves are used fresh or dried. Used mainly with meat and in stuffing.

Mekajiki fillet
This is a swordfish fillet. Swordfish is a very large game fish, 2.5-m long and weighs about 100-500 kg. Its firm flesh is considered excellent and is similar to that of tuna. Swordfish is available fresh or frozen and is best grilled or barbecued.

Mesclun mix salad
A mixture of salad such as lollo rossa, red chicory, frisee, mibuna and others.

Mirin
This liquid flavouring containing 14% alcohol is used in cooking for its sweetness rather than its alcoholic content.

Miso paste
This fermented paste of soy bean and either rice or barley with salt is an essential ingredient in the Japanese larder. It is combined with *dashi* in *miso* soup and also used as a flavouring for other foods.

Mitsukan Suchiro Su
A type of Japanese vinegar.

Mixed herb in oil
A mixture of fresh herbs such as fresh oregano, basil, thyme, majoram, tarragon, rosemary, watercress and English parsley blended with olive oil.

Nameko mushroom
These mushrooms are grown in Japan. They have small brown heads and are grown in clumps. They are mild in flavour and are commonly used in salad, soup and *nabe* dishes.

Ohban yuba
This is made from the skin that forms on the surface of soy milk when heated. It is eaten both fresh or fried. Most *yuba* is made in Kyoto.

Pernod liqueur
An aniseed-flavoured liqueur that is especially useful in cooking fish or seafood dishes.

Pesto crouton
A small piece of bread which is toasted, lightly browned in butter, fried in oil or pesto. Diced croutons are used to garnish certain preparations such as soups, green salads, scrambled eggs, omelettes and butter spinach.

Provolone cheese
A cooked and stretched paste cheese from southern Italy. The plastic curd leads itself to improvisation and Provolone comes in all shapes and sizes.

Ricotta cheese
An Italian curd cheese made from the whey produced as a by-product in the manufacture of various cow's and ewe's milk cheeses. Soft and rindless, with a granular crumbly texture and mild flavour.

Shoyu
Shoyu is a dark brown Japanese soy sauce made from soy beans that have undergone a fermentation process.

Tamari
This type of soy sauce is black with a touch of amber and has a viscous quality. It has a rich, deep flavour and a distinctive, sweet aroma.

Tobiko
This is the roe of the flying fish.

Trenette
Trenette are noodles from Liguria, where they are traditionally served with pesto sauce. They resemble bavette and linguine.

Udon
Available in fresh, precooked and dried forms, these noodles are made from wheat flour. They are paler, softer and thicker than spaghetti. They are often eaten in a bowl of *dashi*-based soup with *tempura* and other accompaniments.

Unagi
Japanese grilled eel.

Usukuchi
Japanese light soy sauce.

White Buna Shimeiji mushroom
This autumn mushroom is known for its excellent flavour rather than its aroma. It has white or straw coloured caps, of about 0.5-cm in diameter.

asian

twist

WEIGHTS & MEASURES

QUANTITIES FOR THIS BOOK ARE GIVEN USING THE METRIC SYSTEM.
STANDARD MEASUREMENTS USED ARE: 1 TSP = 5 ML, 1 DSP = 10 ML, 1 TBSP = 15 ML,
1 CUP = 250 ML. ALL MEASURES ARE LEVEL UNLESS OTHERWISE STATED.

LIQUID AND VOLUME MEASURES

Metric	Imperial	American
5 ml	1/6 fl oz	1 tsp
10 ml	1/3 fl oz	1 dsp
15 ml	1/2 fl oz	1 Tbsp
60 ml	2 fl oz	1/4 cup (4 Tbsp)
85 ml	2 1/2 fl oz	1/3 cup
90 ml	3 fl oz	3/8 cup (6 Tbsp)
125 ml	4 fl oz	1/2 cup
180 ml	6 fl oz	3/4 cup
250 ml	8 fl oz	1 cup
300 ml	10 fl oz (1/2 pint)	1 1/4 cups
375 ml	12 fl oz	1 1/2 cups
435 ml	14 fl oz	1 3/4 cups
500 ml	16 fl oz	2 cups
625 ml	20 fl oz (1 pint)	2 1/2 cups
750 ml	24 fl oz (1 1/5 pints)	3 cups
1 litre	32 fl oz (1 3/5 pints)	4 cups
1.25 litres	40 fl oz (2 pints)	5 cups
1.5 litres	48 fl oz (2 2/5 pints)	6 cups
2.5 litres	80 fl oz (4 pints)	10 cups

DRY MEASURES

Metric	Imperial
30 g	1 ounce
45 g	1 1/2 ounces
55 g	2 ounces
70 g	2 1/2 ounces
85 g	3 ounces
100 g	3 1/2 ounces
110 g	4 ounces
125 g	4 1/2 ounces
140 g	5 ounces
280 g	10 ounces
450 g	16 ounces (1 pound)
500 g	1 pound, 1 1/2 ounces
700 g	1 1/2 pounds
800 g	1 3/4 pounds
1 kg	2 pounds, 3 ounces
1.5 kg	3 pounds, 4 1/2 ounces
2 kg	4 pounds, 6 ounces

OVEN TEMPERATURE

	°C	°F	Gas Regulo
Very slow	120	250	1
Slow	150	300	2
Moderately slow	160	325	3
Moderate	180	350	4
Moderately hot	190/200	370/400	5/6
Hot	210/220	410/440	6/7
Very hot	230	450	8
Super hot	250/290	475/550	9/10

LENGTH

Metric	Imperial
0.5 cm	1/4 inch
1 cm	1/2 inch
1.5 cm	3/4 inch
2.5 cm	1 inch

ABBREVIATION

tsp	teaspoon
Tbsp	tablespoon
g	gram
kg	kilogram
ml	millilitre